Who'$ Driving?

We the People?

"It is rather for us to be here dedicated to the great task remaining before us ... that this nation, under God, shall have a new birth of freedom -- and that government of the people, by the people, for the people, shall not perish from the earth."
Abraham Lincoln

A book of many quotations:
over 200 important quotes by over
100 people of note spanning 2,600 years.

Who'$ Driving?

"We the People?"

Cam Harlan, et al.

Copyright © 2007 by Cam Harlan

Published by   Wimzkl Publishing Company
                      213 Orchard Court
                      Clarkesville, GA 30527.

ISBN: 0-9762553-2-4 (paperback)

ISBN: 0-9762553-3-2 (hard cover)

ISBN: 0-9762553-4-0 (eBook)

Library of Congress Control Number: 2006931706

Printed in the United States of America
Wimzkl Publishing Company

Dedication

Most of all, this book is dedicated to those who we all want to benefit from the greatest public good – our children and theirs and theirs and theirs ... all the generations to come. America is about the children. *"What greater or better gift can we offer the republic than to teach and instruct our youth?"* **Cicero**

This book honors those who, while not individually known, left their grave markers and legacy fighting and dying on the battlefields of liberty: *"To you at home they are columns of figures, or he is a near one who went away and just didn't come back. You didn't see him lying so grotesque and pasty beside the gravel road in France. "We saw him, saw him by the multiple thousands. That's the difference. ..."* -Ernie Pyle

It is also dedicated to the thinkers, strivers, statesmen, and leaders in this world who came together over history in the interest of liberty and made our nation the greatest ever seen in this world *(on the cover and title page, "et al" refers to those quoted throughout this book.)* We must remember and honor them by heeding them. History has repeated itself over and over because history is forgotten. Several, who are quoted, do not deserve to be honored but all need to be remembered. If we forget history, children of the future may just face the horrors of the past.

The list of heroes in the fight for liberty is long and stretches back to antiquity. Not a few were the thinkers and writers who established the philosophical basis for liberty. Some were martyred for the cause. They were mostly common folk although a number came from the aristocracy: Aristotle, John Lilburne, Mary Wollstonecraft, Baron de la Brède et de Montesquieu, Anne-Robert-Jacques Turgot, John Locke, Adam Smith, Benjamin Franklin, Thomas Jefferson, James Madison, Thomas Paine, Alexander Hamilton, Abraham Lincoln, Lord Acton, Henry Ford, Franklin Delano Roosevelt, Winston Churchill, Dietrich Bonhoeffer and Ronald Reagan are pictured. Many more are quoted.

Cover photos: Ronald Reagan and bust of Lord Acton.

Individual columns by Frank Kaiser (suddenlysenior.com) and Randolph T. Holhut (The American Reporter) are quoted.

Other Books by Cam Harlan.

One Day at a Time, Serenity in Rhyme.

This book includes a rhyme for each day of the year having to do with recovery from dysfunction.
ISBN 0-9762553-6-7 e-Book

Nursery Rhymes for Old Farts. (Sample rhymes on page 152)

A collection of amusing reminisces and humor in rhyme.
ISBN 0-9762553-0-8 Soft Cover,
ISBN 0-9762553-1-6 Hard Cover
ISBN 0-9762553-5-9 e-Book

Aim High.

A short biography of the senior, C. Allen Harlan, combined with Cam's autobiography. From a dirt-poor upbringing in Tennessee, Allen's great ambition led him to Detroit where he founded and built one of the largest electrical contracting firms in the country. Later he developed a national reputation as a fundraiser and aided over 3,000 people with their education. He joined the many strivers that have made America great. He loved Detroit and used to say: *"Detroit is where mankind learned how to make enough."* While he could afford a Bentley, he frugally chose to drive a Ford.

Cam, in great contrast, spent most of his life as a golf bum, and chose to drive Porsches. Early on, he displayed great promise and reached significant success, but his ambition was really to win his father's approval. When his father died young, Cam's ambition died with him. He eventually discovered, from an aunt, twenty years too late, that his father was indeed proud of him.

Both C. Allen Harlan and Cam Harlan were poor fathers. C. Allen because he was too busy chasing the American dream and Cam because of clinical depression.
ISBN 0-9762553-8-3 e-Book

Table of Contents

Table of Contents (continued)

Who'$ Driving?

Introduction
Define and Challenge

Definition of a Liberal

TOLERANT
Marked by generosity
OPENHANDED - given or provided in a generous and openhanded way
BROAD-MINDED - not bound by authoritarianism, orthodoxy, or
    traditional forms - not narrow in bounds, opinion or judgment
Demands a balanced and level playing field for all
Wants to take money from the rich and give it to the disadvantaged

Definition of a Conservative

TRADITIONAL
Marked by moderation or caution
Disposed to maintain existing views, conditions, or institutions
MODERATE, CAUTIOUS
Demands a balanced and level playing field for all
Wants to facilitate the flow of wealth upwards through the classes

Definition of an American

TOLERANT
Marked by generosity
OPENHANDED - given or provided in a generous and openhanded way
BROAD-MINDED – not bound by authoritarianism, orthodoxy, or
    traditional forms - not narrow in bounds, opinion or judgment *
TRADITIONAL
Marked by moderation or caution **
Disposed to maintain existing views, conditions, or institutions **
MODERATE, CAUTIOUS
Demands a balanced and level playing field for all to facilitate the
    flow of wealth broadly to those who work and earn.

* Progressive (Liberal) on matters strictly benefiting all the people.
** Conservative on basic American standards, systems and values.

Reader's Challenge: The important quotations next help define
America's conservative standards:

1

Who'$ Driving?

Aristotle: *"The basis of a democratic state is liberty."*
Cicero: *"The welfare of the people is the ultimate law."*
Lord Acton: *"Every class is unfit to govern."*
Dietrich Bonhoeffer: *"The test of the morality of a society is what it does for its children."*
George Santayana: *"Those who cannot remember the past are condemned to repeat it."*
Arnold Toynbee: *"It is a great law of social development that the movement from slavery to freedom is also a movement from security to insecurity of maintenance."*
John Adams: *"Remember, democracy never lasts long. It soon wastes, exhausts, and murders itself. There never was a democracy yet that did not commit suicide."*
Montesquieu: *"Republics end through luxury; monarchies through poverty."*
Plutarch: *"An imbalance between rich and poor is the oldest and most fatal ailment of all republics."*
Will and Ariel Durant: *"Concentration of wealth is a natural result of concentration of ability, and recurs in history. The rate of concentration varies (other factors being equal) with the economic freedom permitted by morals and the law ... democracy, allowing the most liberty, accelerates it."*
Ronald Reagan: *"Freedom is special and rare. It's fragile; it needs protection."*
Abraham Lincoln: *"It is rather for us to be here dedicated to the great task remaining before us ... that this nation, under God, shall have a new birth of freedom -- **and that government of the people, by the people, for the people, <u>shall not</u> <u>perish from the earth.</u>"***

These words are remembered with good cause. You, as the reader, are challenged to make an evaluation as to their validity. **Please give each quotation your serious consideration.** The observations and conclusions made in this book find foundation in these among other quotations. As with any beliefs, you may disagree for whatever reason; however, these quotes have withstood the test of time.

If you doubt any, make very sure that you are not finding disbelief because you *"know better in your gut."* History says that liberty will be lost at some date in the future, even here in America (see Adams quote.) Disagreement based on *"in the gut"* beliefs may hasten the process (see Santayana quote.)

2

Who'$ Driving?

Do you believe in Liberty?
Do you believe in the "Separation of Powers?
Do you believe in capitalism?"
Do you believe the problem is the government?

The problem is not the government itself. It is the politicians and it is even more the powerful "persons" and their lobbyists financing the election and incumbency of the politicians! The problem is **"Who'$ Driving?" Is it "We the People?"**

Because of our unique and ingenious Constitution, America has an outside chance of surviving as a democracy. Our Founding Fathers were aware of the history that brought an end to all democracies so we must remember that history and make very sure the conditions causing previous failures do not reoccur. If we remember history and maintain a level and balanced playing field for all, liberty in America can survive.

Why should anyone believe there is any realistic threat to liberty? It is a risk/reward judgment. Since every historic democracy came to an end falling to concentrated political power, history's repetitiousness says ours will as well. Because there is very little chance of America falling to some outside political power now, the only realistic threat is internal concentrated political power. The risk now may or may not be great, but that risk will increase over time especially if the imbalance found in the concentration of wealth continues. This is not a derogation of wealth since wealth is the key motivational factor that makes capitalism work. It is concern over significant imbalance – see Plutarch quote.

Your decision should be made based on the risk in the future. **You must ask yourself if you are willing to risk the liberty of America's children 50, 100 or 200 years from now or ever.** Could the Romans of 100BC foresee the events of 30BC? You must weigh the rewards of your present political beliefs against the risk Reagan spoke of when he said: "There is only an up or down - up to man's age-old dream - the ultimate in individual freedom consistent with law and order - or down to the ant heap of totalitarianism, those who would trade our freedom for security have embarked on this downward course."

You should conclude that it is a risk we must not take! In the words of Plato: *"The price of apathy towards public affairs is to be ruled by evil men."* Many great thinkers regard democracy as the most unstable political system because of an inherent potential for imbalance – see Plutarch and the Durants quotes above. Refer to Lincoln's quote often – it is most critical *"that government of the people, by the people, for the people, <u>shall not perish from the earth.</u>"*

3

Who'$ Driving?

Chapter One
"on the right track."

John Lilburne, 1615-1657

John Lilburne was born in England and became known as *"Freeborn John"* to his countrymen. Rights were usually regarded as those bestowed by governments, but he claimed everyman was born with *"freeborn rights."* John was an active politician and came in conflict with King Charles I over these rights. He also clashed with Oliver Cromwell. who was a military dictator for some time. We derive our phrase *"inalienable rights"* from his writings. We believe as a *"self evident truth"* that all men are *"endowed by their Creator with certain unalienable Rights"*.

Too often in our adulthood, we are caught up in ideas that we regard as the absolute truth. We learn from predecessors their beliefs and become prejudiced in those beliefs. Such prejudiced knowledge is that, regardless of the subject, believed to be the absolute truth.

Inalienable has replaced *"unalienable"* in modern dictionaries. It is, indeed, an interesting and, perhaps, revered word in America as we all accept the concept that humans are born with certain inalienable rights. There are, however, many and various other ideas that may become inalienable as a practical matter. Some of these are political and religious teachings which are accepted by the believers as absolute truth being the party line or the *"Word of God!"* No amount of argument, factual information or sometimes force can alter *"in the gut"* beliefs. Often in the past, humans have sacrificed their bodies and lives for their beliefs, like John Lilburne who spent considerable time in prison and had an eye pierced by a pike for his, then liberal, now conservative views.

Thus, we have given some religious and political leaders the opportunity to control the lives of others through the creation of inalienable fabrications. These distortions must, of course, be reasonable or have some plausible historic foundation in order to reach the level of inalienability, but they can conflict directly with our basic conservative values. Equally and, perhaps, even more importantly, they must be something people want to believe. Michel Eyquem de Montaigne said: **"Nothing is so firmly believed as what we least know."**

4

Who'$ Driving?

Unfortunately, prejudiced knowledge usually blocks out opposing opinions. A neighbor of the author, when confronted about the merits of modern day corporations said: *"I don't want to hear it"* and repeated it several times. He is unwilling to even listen to anything that might challenge his beliefs. Another neighbor, who had agreed to read and critique this book, changed his mind after reading an early draft of one chapter, declining to proceed because: *"You are attacking everything I have believed all my life."* Minds closed by *"in the gut"* knowledge.

There is a statue of a woman in Boston Common who was hung by other Christians for espousing Quaker beliefs – four Quakers were hung in Boston between 1659 and 1661. America's Bill of Rights was conceived and enacted to protect the rights of minorities in order to avoid or minimize the social damage resulting from prejudiced knowledge; and so, we have mostly learned to live peacefully together here in America.

Liberty, our most precious possession, does not just involve the right to do as one pleases within the boundaries of law; it is also the right to make free, informed choices without undue influence from others. We bewail the fact that so many Moslem youngsters are being raised with heavy emphasis on certain teachings of the Quran because it seems to birth suicide bombers. Don't we all really agree that governments should not interfere with religion and religions must keep out of politics?

A few years ago, in Ireland, Catholics nailed a protestant to a fence. Here in America, we still have Christian fanatics who blow up buildings, attack abortion clinics and homosexuals. Acts self-justified by their *"in the gut"* inalienable beliefs. We now have politicians seeking and in office who belong to and cater to the religious right as their means to office. Few will recognize this as a threat to liberty but all should. It is unique in American and European cultures that many competing religions prevent any single religion from establishing a monopoly. The result is religious liberty for all. Lord Acton said: ***"The most certain test by which we judge whether a country is really free is the amount of security enjoyed by minorities."*** Do we all not want our children to have the security found in freedom of religion?

Julius Caesar said: ***"Men readily believe what they want to believe,"*** and, people do want to believe. It is part of the patriotic feeling. *"Deutschland, Deutschland, Uber Alles!"* Remember how the German people embraced Hitler. *"My country 'tis of thee, sweet land of liberty"* is similar, yet significantly different. Leaders often are revered and their shortcomings dismissed. Mistakes (Viet Nam,) dishonesty (Nixon) and even immorality (Clinton) can be ignored or pardoned. If the reasons for an action are proved invalid (Iraq,) then other reasons can be found to re-rationalize the action.

Many elections are won and lost based solely on slogans – *"war on crime," "war on terror," "contract with America,"* etc. Emotions become the guiding force and moderates need to question such emotions. Frank Layden, Utah Jazz president, on a former player said: *"I told him, 'Son, what is it with you? Is it ignorance or apathy?' He said, 'Coach, I don't know, and I don't care.'"* Many conservatives and liberals don't know history and, worse, don't care; and that is truly scary.

There is enormous pressure on elective officials involved in their election and their incumbency. **Because of this pressure, both the Republicans and the Democrats leadership must be considered Not Conservative.** Both parties respond to pressure for special legislation favoring those that provide their election financing and that removes any hope the voters may have for a smaller, practical and frugal government. **If the historic and immoral additions to the national debt by the party in power are an indication of a party's conservatism, then both parties are liberal and the Republicans are, by far, the most liberal.**

James Madison said: *"The truth is that all men having power ought to be mistrusted."* We all do so want to believe that America is the greatest, but that does not mean America can do no wrong. Upstanding Germans believed and Hitler's intolerance and arrogance caused much wrong. While the occasional statesman may be humble, political leadership, seemingly by nature, is arrogant. Kissinger called it *"the American temptation toward perfection and the absolute."* We must always question and distrust power.

H. L. Mencken said: *"Under democracy, one party always devotes its chief energies to trying to prove that the other party is unfit to rule, and both commonly succeed, and are right."*

Conservatives and Liberals *"want to believe"* and have a strong sense of loyalty to the Party of their choice. At the same time, they know the *"country is not on the right track"* so the natural conclusion is that fault must lie the other side. **Our *"temptation toward perfection and the absolute"* has created an impenetrable wall between the two sides.**

The present circumstances which allow an elastic and unlimited government can be traced directly to FDR and Ronald Reagan. Thus, both sides are finding fault correctly while denying their own complicity. **If America is going to get back "on the right track," we need to find more precise definitions as to what exactly we are, what our standards are and what our goal is.**

6

Who'$ Driving?

Chapter Two
General Welfare

Benjamin Franklin (1706-1790)

The importance for Americans of the *"General Welfare"* is basic since it appears twice in the Constitution: First in the Preamble which is not a delegation of power to the federal government; it is the stated goal of our nation. Then in Article 1, Section 8: *"The Congress shall have Power to lay and collect Taxes, Duties, Imposts and Excises, to pay the Debts and provide for the common Defense and general Welfare of the United States; but all Duties, Imposts and Excises shall be uniform throughout the United States."*

What constitutes the *"General Welfare"* is a contentious issue that has plagued America from the start. Benjamin Franklin proposed its inclusion since the Second Continental Congress was in danger of failing due to petty disagreements over minor issues. It was left to Franklin and a few others to direct their energies toward broader issues. James Madison prodded the members of the Convention that they were *"framing a system which we wish to last for ages."* Alexander Hamilton: *"... concurred with Mr. Madison in thinking we were now to decide for ever the fate of Republican Government; and that if we did not give to that form due stability and wisdom, it would be disgraced & lost among ourselves, disgraced & lost to mankind for ever."*

In recent years, the political divisions seen in America are the direct descendent of the dispute over the meaning of *"General Welfare."* Many of the Founders adopted a *"nationalist"* stance for a strong government empowered to promote economic growth. Early on, the battle over a national bank reflected this contention. The corrupt and failed managing of the First National Bank added to the dispute.

The Civil War, as well, reflected the disagreement as seen in the absence of a *"General Welfare"* clause in the Confederate Constitution of 1861. In the last century, the bone most hard to swallow for those on the right was the New Deal. The Court's liberalization of the meaning of

7

"General Welfare" which allowed the implementation of the New Deal was necessitated, rightly or wrongly, by *"a crisis so extreme"* – the Great Depression. This basic revision can be laid right on FDR and is the reason conservatives hold him and the New Deal in such low esteem. This makes him no less one of our greatest leaders. This liberalization is a corruption of the intended meaning of the *"General Welfare."*

Alexander Hamilton (1755-1804)

Hamilton specifically stated that Federal funds could not be applied to the welfare of a single state or locale: *"The constitutional test of a right application must always be, whether it be for a purpose of general or local nature. If the former, there can be no want of constitutional power.... Whatever relates to the general order of the finances, to the general interests of trade etc., being general objects are constitutional ones for the application of money."*

Still Hamilton did feel that the *"General Welfare"* included the broad areas of education, agriculture, manufacturing and commerce: *"To cherish and stimulate the activity of the human mind, by multiplying the objects of enterprise, is not among the least considerable of the expedients, by which the wealth of a nation may be promoted.... Every new scene which is opened to the busy nature of man to rouse and exert itself, is the addition of a new energy to the general stock of effort."*

Hamilton favored aggressive policies to promote manufacturing and commerce including import quotas, tariffs and export prohibitions of raw materials needed in domestic manufacturing. He also wanted federal standard of measures, programs to facilitate shipping of products and a banking system for reliable payments. He maintained there could be no better purpose *"to which public money can be more beneficially applied than to the acquisition of a new and useful branch of industry; no Consideration more valuable than a permanent addition to the general stock of productive labor."*

Hamilton believed the legislature must determine what constitutes the *"General Welfare,"* when he said: *"And there seems to be no room for a doubt that whatever concerns the general interests of Learning, of Agriculture, of Manufactures, and of Commerce, are within the sphere of the national Councils, as far as regards an application of money."*

James Madison expressed limitations: *"With respect to the words general welfare, I have always regarded them as qualified by the detail of powers connected with them. To take them in a literal and unlimited sense would be a metamorphosis of the Constitution into a character which there is a host of proofs was not contemplated by its creators."* Thomas Jefferson concurred: *"Congress has not unlimited powers to provide for the general welfare, but only those specifically enumerated."*

Most of the Founding Fathers believed that the Federal Government had to be empowered to promote the *"General Welfare."* Washington assented in this belief as did John Marshall, the first Chief Justice of the Supreme Court. He said: *"But when, 'In order to form a more perfect union,' it was deemed necessary to change this alliance into an effective government, possessing great and sovereign powers, and acting directly upon the people; the necessity of referring it to the people, and of deriving its power directly from them, was felt and acknowledged by all. The government of the Union, then ... is emphatically and truly a government of the people. In form and in substance it emanates from them, its powers are granted by them, and are to be exercised directly on them, and for their benefit. Let the end be legitimate, let it be within the scope of the Constitution, and all means which are appropriate, which are plainly adapted to that end, which are not prohibited, but consist with the letter and spirit of the Constitution, are constitutional...."*

Many believe Abraham Lincoln derived inspiration from this quote. **"Government of the people, by the people and for the people," has great bearing on the contentious issue of the *"General Welfare."***

The Supreme Court in 1937 affirmed two New Deal programs based on the *"General Welfare"* clause. Both had to do with the Social Security Act - old age benefits and unemployment tax and benefits. The vast majority of Americans accept these pay-as-you-go programs as justified by the *"General Welfare"* clause of the Constitution.

Many other New Deal programs termed the "Three Rs," more or less, met the same test. **Relief** for the one-third of the population hardest hit by the depression. These were termed *"appropriate responses to the critical situation"* by Milton Friedman. **Recovery** involved programs to restore the economy to normal health. These were working by 1937, although unemployment continued high until World War II began. **Reform**, predicated on a belief in the inherent instability of the market included the Wagner Act encouraging labor unions. The TVA alone involved government ownership of the means of production – satisfying a regional public need private enterprise would not address. A majority of economists criticized some of these *"Reform"* programs.

Supreme Court interpretation of the "General Welfare" was recast in *US vs. Butler* (1936) when the Agricultural Adjustment Act was voided. The Court adopted the view that *"General Welfare"* is a grant of congressional authority based broadly on the spending power. Since all governmental activity involves the expenditure of money; **the *"General Welfare"* Clause became a plenary grant of power.**

Compounding this problem is Clause 18, also in Section 8, known as the *"necessary and proper"* clause. Often referred to as the *"elastic"* clause, it goes hand-in-hand with the *"General Welfare"* clause, stating: *"To make all Laws which shall be necessary and proper for carrying into Execution the foregoing Powers, and all other Powers vested by this Constitution in the Government of the United States, or in any Department or Officer thereof."* *"Forgoing Powers"* refers to the 17 previous clauses strictly defining Congressional powers.

This clause was cited in a 1976 case (Buckley vs. Valeo) in which the Supreme Court upheld public financing of Presidential elections. The Court stated: *"Congress was legislating for the `general welfare'--to reduce the deleterious influence of large contributions on our political process, to facilitate communication by the candidates with the electorate, and to free candidates from the rigors of fundraising."*

The opponents of the campaign financing law maintained there were insufficient constitutional grounds. The liberal Supremes found (5 to 4) that the *"General Welfare"* clause is not a limitation on the power of Congress: ***"It is rather a grant of power, the scope of which is quite expansive, particularly in view of the enlargement of power by the Necessary and Proper Clause."***

In opening this can of worms, the terms *"liberal and conservative"* took on new political meanings and we now have a confusion of these terms. **Conservatives now have authority to spend liberally and they do just that.** As James Madison said: *"If Congress can do whatever in their discretion can be done by money, and will promote the General Welfare, the Government is no longer a limited one, possessing enumerated powers, but an indefinite one, subject to particular exceptions."* He also said: *"I cannot undertake to lay my finger on that article of the Constitution which granted a right to Congress of expending, on objects of benevolence, the money of their constituents."*

Who'$ Driving?

People now on the right support the Republican Party and know that FDR was one of the *"bad"* guys - it was the New Deal leading to ruin - but they may not know why. They do not recognize that the court decisions allowing the New Deal now **allow unlimited fiscal liberalism.**

Conservative leaders, while posturing to limited government, have become the most liberal spenders. Liberal leaders join in with a slightly different agenda.. The confrontation between liberal and conservative is over the source of funds (both tax revenue and campaign financing) and expenditures and has birthed an animosity that has effectively ended practical dialog between the two. Unhappily, we now have legions of lobbyists dictating what satisfies the *"General Welfare"* clause and our political leadership make it into law with seemingly little question. **The standards that are fundamentally conservative for Americans are being buried under a liberal and *"elastic"* government.**

Cicero describing Rome's equivalent of our lobbyists, said: *"A nation can survive its fools, and even the ambitious. But it cannot survive treason from within. An enemy at the gates is less formidable, for he is known and he carries his banners openly. But the traitor moves among those within the gate freely, his sly whispers rustling through all the alleys, heard in the very halls of government itself. For the traitor appears no traitor; he speaks in accents familiar to his victims, and he wears their face and their garments, and he appeals to the baseness that lies deep in the hearts of all men. He rots the soul of a nation; he works secretly and unknown in the night to undermine the pillars of a city; he infects the body politic so that it can no longer resist. A murderer is less to be feared."*

Sageisms: *A made-up word of obvious meaning. While many of these come from antiquity, they all deserve your thought and consideration.*

"For with primacy in power is also joined an awe inspiring accountability to the future." -Winston Churchill

"Nothing doth more hurt in a state than that cunning men pass for wise." -Sir Francis Bacon

"We have some real political differences among us, but we all share the same goals: clean air and water, injury free workplaces, safe transportation systems, to name a few of the good things that can come from regulation." -Fred Thompson

Chapter Three
Tale of two - twice

There are many things that can harm our system. One is having a President indifferent to the desires of the populous; which may be the case with George W. Bush. In six years, Mr. Bush has vetoed one bill saying that an embryonic stem-cell research bill *"crossed a moral boundary."* His judgment repudiates the will of the majority who see stem-cell research as having important medical possibilities. He continues to display minimal fiscal conservatism and ignores the widespread opposition to war. He decries withdrawal from Iraq as "losing." The threat of terrorism in America is thwarted by our enormous military capability to wipe out governments. Is it thwarted by trying to maintain order in a nation as religiously and politically divided as Iraq?

The divisions in America widen because of this <u>not conservative</u> propensity to ignore the will of the people and our basic conservative standards. But these divisions precede Mr. Bush and can be traced back to two very popular Presidents. One, Franklin Delano Roosevelt, is the inspiration of the left leaving a legacy with the New Deal and spawning many social programs. The other, Ronald Reagan significantly moved the intellect and emotions of those on the right. Both men are icons.

Why are FDR and Ronald Reagan regarded by many as great Presidents and reviled by others as bringing ultimate potential ruin on our great nation? In the last hundred years, there are probably no other two men who created greater controversy among the voting citizens of America. Both were loved by most and thoroughly hated by many.

Both took us successfully through times of great danger. Roosevelt guided us through the Great Depression, maintaining capitalism, and World War II, maintaining liberty. Regan brought an end to the Cold War and help guide Russia from being a serious threat into being a benign partner, making the world a safer place.

Both men were true Americans with the *"General Welfare"* of the whole populace as their guiding light. Both were sincere, honest men bringing high ideals to our highest office. Both were apparently in touch with the ultimate needs of the nation in times of great danger, and both had a deep regard for our standards and our history. Both men listened to the people and understood what the public wants and what America is about – the children and the future.

Both made grave errors posing long term potential threats to our most treasured standards. Neither FDR nor Reagan could foresee that implementation of their policies could ultimately threaten our basic liberties by contributing to an *"elastic"* government. Both had the agreement and support of a majority of other political leaders, expert advisers and the American public.

Yet, it is just these errors that split the nation into supporting and detracting camps that have polarized the political world. It is in these errors that we now face the *"up or down"* Reagan spoke of in his farewell speech: *"up to man's age-old dream - the ultimate in individual freedom consistent with law and order - or down to the ant heap of totalitarianism, those who would trade our freedom for security have embarked on this downward course."*

Roosevelt's threat to *"pack the Court"* in order to implement his New Deal programs apparently coerced the Supremes into liberalizing the interpretation of the *"General Welfare"* clause. As James Madison predicted: *"If Congress can do whatever in their discretion can be done by money, and will promote the General Welfare, the Government is no longer a limited one, possessing enumerated powers, but an indefinite one, subject to particular exceptions."* **We now have unlimited government in a nation that demands limited government.** This can lead *"down to the ant heap of totalitarianism."*

Reagan's implementation of "Supply Side" economic theory has proved equally threatening because political leaders, falsely claiming to be conservative, continue using it to create a dangerous imbalance in our society. **It became not just okay to implement policies favoring the rich and powerful, Reagan made it desirable,** thereby accelerating the concentration of wealth. Together, Reagan and Roosevelt created a political world where the term *"conservative"* lost traditional meaning.

Supply Side could have been implemented without the liberalization of *"General Welfare,"* but the growing lobbyist impact and the sheer size of the government probably could not have occurred. Government subject only to *"particular exceptions"* does not, in any way, satisfy the demands of America's conservative standards. **Can America survive with an *"indefinite"* government?** America needs to return to the standards and values that lead *"up to man's age-old dream - the ultimate in individual freedom consistent with law and order."*

Lobbyists have gradually and covertly distorted the meaning of *"conservative."* As Cicero said: *"He rots the soul of a nation; he works secretly and unknown in the night to undermine the pillars of a city; he infects the body politic so that it can no longer resist. A murderer is less to be feared."*

Who'$ Driving?

Illustrating the split in our political camps is the tale of two other men who bear the same name and were relatives of the author. Both were Associate Justices of the Supreme Court, both were Republicans and each was known in his own time as *"the great dissenter."*

On a conservative Court for 33 years, John Marshall Harlan stood alone as *"the great dissenter"* against then liberal interpretations of the Reconstruction, particularly the 14th, Amendments. While the Court was moving away from protecting former slaves, he wrote eloquent dissents in favor of equal rights not just for African Americans but for all Americans.

He was a slave-owner from Kentucky, and while the Emancipation Proclamation did not free his slaves, he contractually freed them himself. In 1896, the Supreme Court handed down in *Plessy vs. Ferguson,* a decision establishing the doctrine of *"separate but equal"* Southern segregation practices. Harlan dissented: *"But in view of the constitution, in the eye of the law, there is in this country no superior, dominant, ruling class of citizens. There is no caste here. **Our constitution is color-blind, and neither knows nor tolerates classes among citizens.** In respect of civil rights, all citizens are equal before the law. The humblest is the peer of the most powerful. The law regards man as man, and takes no account of his surroundings or of his color when his civil rights as guaranteed by the supreme law of the land are involved."*

His grandson, John Marshall Harlan II served from 1955 to 1971. He also was termed *"the great dissenter,"* but as a conservative on a liberal Court. Harlan II believed that most problems should be solved by the political process, and that the judiciary should play only a limited role – (don't we all?) He wrote: *"These decisions give support to a current mistaken view of the Constitution and the constitutional function of this court. This view, in a nutshell, is that every major social ill in this country can find its cure in some constitutional principle and that this court should take the lead in promoting reform when other branches of government fail to act. The Constitution is not a panacea for every blot upon the public welfare nor should this court, ordained as a judicial body, be thought of as a general haven of reform movements."*

These two are cited here, not from family pride, but to underline the point that the meanings of conservative and liberal have blurred. There was great similarity between Grandfather and Grandson especially as concerned the *"due process clause"* of the Fourteenth Amendment. Both were *"great dissenters"* but from opposite sides because the term *"conservative"* lost meaning at the top levels of political power. Like most Americans, both wanted a balanced and level playing field for all.

14

Chapter Four
Up or down

Dietrich Bonhoeffer 1906-1945

As a writer and theologian, Dr. Bonhoffer was summarily hanged in the Flossenburg concentration camp only weeks before the end of World War II for spearheading a Protestant resistance movement against Adolph Hitler and the Nazis. He displayed enormous courage standing up for his religious and moral beliefs: **"The test of the morality of a society is what it does for its children."** That is why Americans demand a balanced and level playing field for all.

America's <u>Conservative</u> <u>Standards</u> must be maintained for the children of the future:

General Welfare is America's goal.

Liberty is a Human **Condition** – mankind's inalienable right.

Democracy and Capitalism - America's **Systems** of human activity.

Separation of Powers and separation of church and state are America's **Systems** protecting liberty, democracy and capitalism.

Patriotism, Morality, Frugality, Practicality, Balance, and a limited government honoring the sanctity of privacy are America's six **Values** defining and limiting democratic and capitalistic systems.

John Locke wrote: *"Men being...by nature all free, equal and independent, no one can be put out of his estate and subjected to the political power of another without his own consent which is done by agreeing with other men, to join and unite into a community for their comfortable, safe, and peaceable living...in a secure enjoyment of their properties..."* Our Founding Fathers found inspiration in these words.

Government *"of the people, by the people, for the people"* is to insure our **condition** of liberty, and the basic conservative *systems* based on the communal *values* of the citizens. **All government programs, then, must fit into the** *systems* **and satisfy the** *values.* **The** *values* **must be paramount and protect** *liberty* **while insuring** *privacy.*

What exactly do you want to conserve? Pay close heed to the greats of history quoted in this book. They tell us why these values are under threat, what endangers them, and why we must conserve them. The danger to our standards is recognized by few because *"Those who cannot remember the past are condemned to repeat it,"* (George Santayana) and because too many have learned, inalienable beliefs.

The six communal conservative values are too often ignored by our political and corporate leadership. A strict interpretation of *"General Welfare"* indicates it must be uniform throughout the United States. **We now have a** **not conservative** **interpretation that has violated our limited government value, split America politically and engendered a fiscal imbalance that threatens America's conservative standards.**

Ronald Reagan in a speech supporting Barry Goldwater's candidacy for President in 1964 said: *"You and I are told increasingly that we have to choose between a left or right, but* **I would like to suggest that there is no such thing as a left or right. There is only an up or down** *- up to man's age-old dream - the ultimate in individual freedom consistent with law and order - or down to the ant heap of totalitarianism, those who would trade our freedom for security have embarked on this downward course."*

The only worthwhile dialog among us should be to determine what government programs sustain balance, the *"general welfare"* and our common conservative standards. This leads *"up."* Both liberals and conservatives arrogantly wear their labels too proudly; all the time *"preaching to the choir"* and this lack of dialog leads *"down."*

The majority of Americans are moderates who love their liberties, desire minimal governmental interference, and believe in the community of America wanting what is right and best for all the people and, especially, for our children. This surely contrasts to the authoritarian *"arrogance of officialdom"* (Cicero) by leaders of both parties whose actions often imply indifference to our conservative standards.

Moderates may or may not be liberal or conservative, Republicans or Democrats. These labels have lost specific meaning. **Is not America a pragmatic nation embracing the revolutionary when need requires, but demanding as little government as possible?** That government must embrace Cicero's wisdom when he said: *"The welfare of the people is the ultimate law"* by reasserting a strict interpretation of the *"General Welfare"* clause and insuring a level and balanced playing field.

16

Chapter Five
Balance

Throughout this book, you will find references to balance. It is a common word used often in all our lives. Balance can bring joy. Picture a baby finding balance in first steps. Remember the thrill of watching a wire balancing act, dangerously high. The romance found in a dance; the fun in climbing a tree; the enthusiasm watching a closely contested athletic match; and the comfort of a happy family. Balance is a core; it is demanded and demanding; satisfying; everywhere and meaningful.

Imbalance comes naturally with age in people, societies and corporations. History is the record of social imbalance. Imbalance in the body is pain, sickness and death. Imbalance in genes can be devastating. Imbalance in appearance or talent yields movie stars and outcasts. Imbalance in mental abilities can yield success or failure. Imbalance in population demographics can yield discrimination even to the point of hatred and terrorism. Imbalance yields winners and losers.

Winning and losing is what life is about, yet we demand rules and regulations for balance. One person or group or team may dominate, but then, nature comes into play. That person or group or team will age and fall by the wayside. **Nature abhors any imbalance. Man abhors any playing field that is not level.** Let the best win, but make sure the laws, rules and circumstances favor no one over another.

Most people are convinced that professional athletes take drugs that enhance performance. They don't like it and think drug tests should be mandatory because they want balance. Many hate the Yankees because their payroll is more than double the average and six times the lowest. They disapprove but understand both the drugs and the payroll since they appreciate that it is only human to want an unbalanced advantage.

While nature abhors imbalance, it is found everywhere. There is a top and bottom of the food chain. There are big predators and small. There is talent and slow. There is aggression and timidity. There are jocks and geeks. There is the able and the disable. Imbalance is found in individuals and groups. Balance has nothing to do with fair. Balance is and must be impersonal, but it is always critical.

When the balance of cells in a human body is corrupted by cancer cells, the whole community of cells suffers and may die. When you have a large city of peaceful citizens working together, that balance can be seriously damaged by terrorists. The terrorists may come from outside, or they may just be a dissatisfied lower class. The community suffers.

17

Who'$ Driving?

In our political system, we have *"Checks and Balances"* among the most important standards. They were instituted by our Founding Fathers because man was created equal. Balance ensures equality and harmony and works for all. The standards of our nation that we most want to conserve were conceived to insure balance.

If some one segment of our societal system becomes unbalanced, like cancer cells, it jeopardizes the whole. When the whole is balanced, it can grow and prosper with confidence. And so we have grown and prospered. And we are confident. It is the American way.

We are now a nation of over 300 million people. We have great disparity and much inequality in many ways, but we make the inequality work for us in capitalism. Capitalism, by its very nature, must be a system of imbalance. But, like nature, it is a system of imbalance that is supposed to work toward balance. Free markets are competitive and competition fulfills consumers' needs on the best terms; all the while yielding profit and justified, unequal wealth for strivers.

We applaud the strivers and reward them as they should be rewarded. Our list of national heroes includes Henry Ford, Andrew Carnegie, Thomas Edison, George Westinghouse and Bill Gates among the long list of inventors and innovators that gave us so much that makes life so much easier. But they didn't just give it to us, they sold it to us and we bought it. They inspired the desire, and we made the purchase

Our system develops, produces and delivers to the consumer. If the consumer buys, the system grows. Most investment comes from profits. It costs so much to manufacture any product - the materials used are consumed from other manufacturers whereby those others make profits. All manufacturers pay for labor. When you sell your products, you may make a profit which can be reinvested and more growth can follow. But the product must be sold. It all comes down to the consumer.

The greatest economic growth ever seen was the result of an expanding, prosperous, spending middle class. This is basic economics. There is no question of which came first, the chicken or the egg. Banking actually predates the invention of coin money – receipts for stored grain and other commodities were circulated. These could be invested, but the demand and trade of the commodities preceded both banking and money.

The needs came first. In antiquity, it was satisfied by hunters and gatherers. When profits, partially in the form of leisure time, arose, man was able to create implements and tools facilitating hunting, gathering and consuming. Invention and innovation always require consumption. When there is too much production without consumption, the system becomes unbalanced. These exact conditions of imbalance were the root cause of the Great Depression. The misery of that event is forgotten.

Basic capitalistic theory says you cannot have excess production for long, but history has proved that it can not only happen, the resulting imbalance can be devastating for the economic system. It is like a cancerous growth when there is excess production not balanced by a growing ability to consume by the populous. How could you have excess production without a concurrent growth in the ability to consume? It happened because capitalism depends on free markets. Normally, when you have excess production, the lack of demand will cause prices to fall until there is sufficient demand. In the 1920's, prices were not subject to free market pressure because the market was not free. .

Prices were set and kept high by a small number of enormous corporations – only a few survive. This imbalance was the result of many factors but primarily from the rise and domination of corporations in our economic system. The dominance of corporations and the definition of *"General Welfare"* may be the most critical issues dividing the conservatives and liberals. Conservatives love Corporate America and revel in its successes. They ignore its inevitable failures and have little knowledge of its history – this book is a reminder of that history.

Huge corporations are inherently imbalanced. Efficiency in size is a myth because the depth of management, like all bureaucracies, can reach a point where top managers lose touch with the large numbers of people below them. When profit becomes the only goal, management can and has lost touch with basic moral standards.

A small businessman will strive and succeed, but then he will age, become set in his ways and slow down. Henry Ford lost dominance to GM - a more youthful striver with new and different ideas including growth by purchase of competitors. Both used a corporate charter; which use has been corrupted from its original purpose. We now have immortal *"persons"* in the business world. That doesn't mean they will be successful forever – virtually none are. It means the playing field is no longer balanced. Part of that is size and part is the lack of barriers to buying out competition. Part is that huge corporations do not play by normal capitalistic rules. David rarely can defeat Goliath.

Even Adam Smith reached the same conclusion in "The Wealth of Nations:" *"A monopoly granted either to an individual or to a trading company has the same effect as a secret in trade or manufactures. The monopolists, by keeping the market constantly understocked, by never fully supplying the effectual demand, sell their commodities much above the natural price, and raise their emoluments, whether they consist in wages or profit, greatly above their natural rate. The price of monopoly is upon every occasion the highest which can be got. The natural price, or the price of free competition, on the contrary, is the lowest which can be taken, not upon every occasion, indeed, but for any considerable time together. The one is upon every occasion the highest which can be squeezed out of the buyers, or which, it is supposed, they will consent to give: the other is the lowest which the sellers can commonly afford to take, and at the same time continue their business.*

"The **exclusive privileges of corporations***, statutes of apprenticeship, and all those laws which restrain, in particular employments, the competition to a smaller number than might otherwise go into them, have the same tendency, though in a less degree. They are a sort of enlarged monopolies, and may frequently, for ages together, and in whole classes of employments, keep up the market price of particular commodities above the natural price, and maintain both the wages of the labor and the profits of the stock employed about them somewhat above their natural rate. Such enhancements of the market price may last as long as the regulations of police which give occasion to them."* Many historians consider Adam Smith the father of capitalism and *"The Wealth of Nations:"* his most inspirational work.

There are economists who argue that investment and production is the key to economic growth, citing as evidence the fact that great consuming countries are the great producing countries, ignoring the fact that great producing countries are the great consuming countries. By exporting so much of our production, America is rapidly disproving that premise. Those economists go on to claim that any economic policy focusing on consumption rather than investment will eventually lower purchasing power. An analysis of recent trends in economic growth and the growth in consumption discredits that theory as well. Profits and savings are the result of investment and production only when and if there is compensation in consumption.

You may believe there is no *"exclusive privileges"* of corporations. If there is not, why are there so many lobbyists in Washington representing corporations? Why allow corporations to move charters overseas to avoid taxation? How did Chrysler get $1 billion in Federal loan guarantees to avoid bankruptcy? Why can Americans not purchase drugs from Canada? Why can student loans be refinanced only once?

It is a lot worse than that. Our government has catered to some of the worst dictators ever known. One must suspect this is in response to private interests wanting to do business in those markets. The list is long: Augusto Pinochet, "Papa Doc" Duvalier, Rafael Trujillos, Fulgencio Batista, and Anastasio Somoza just in the Western hemisphere. We continue to support many others around the world, particularly oil producers. This is not the American way. We are in Iraq because we want liberty for all and we abhor violation of human rights.

Perhaps Arnold Toynbee expressed it best when he wrote: *"America is today the leader of a world-wide anti-revolutionary movement in the defense of vested interests. She now stands for what Rome stood for. Rome consistently supported the rich against the poor in all foreign communities that fell under her sway; and, since the poor, so far, have always and everywhere been far more numerous than the rich, Rome's policy made for inequality, for injustice, and for the least happiness of the greatest number."*

Such inequality can only be maintained by force. It is the ultimate and most obnoxious form of imbalance. The corporate managers who work in oil nations may see imbalance, but they are lower level and have no say in corporate policy. Top management deals with those controlling from the top and while they may care, their job is about profits.

This is America, the most giving and caring nation that the World has ever seen. How can people not care about liberty and human rights? How is it that profits sometimes become the sole motivation? Is it because these powerful people are transitory? They will only be there for a while, and the corporation, maybe, will go on and on. Immortals have neither soul nor conscience – they have only purpose. Corporations are *"persons"* in the eyes of the law and this should not be the case.

It does not matter how many millions own the stocks of these immortal corporations; if the small number of managers are dishonest, incompetent or mistaken, huge numbers of people suffer. The vast majority of stockholders have no significant political power. Imbalance is too much power in too few hands, which also breeds the danger of corruption and immorality. Could any small company with 30 or 300 or 3,000 employees, buy government favors to gain an advantage over competition? Could any of the millions of small businessmen in America? Some big corporations can and do all the time.

Not conservative policies create imbalance in *"exclusive privileges."* Many of the important people involved in the inspiration, creation and maintenance of the American system have warned of the danger of corporations, but man forgets history. We live in a fragile democracy requiring balance and a level playing field. Who's driving?

21

Who'$ Driving?

Chapter Six
American community

America is a nation of communities and communal activities are a basic part of our culture. Early on, when the barn of a neighbor was destroyed by fire, the whole community would come together in "barn raising." Such activity was voluntary; but it was considered and treated as a moral obligation on the part of all citizens. When urban centers reached a size allowing hired public services, this burden was transferred from direct participation to tax supported systems.

Communal services were extensive and included schools, libraries, police, fire, emergency, social and medical services. Such community activities continue to this day as do electric membership corporations and Habitat for Humanity. Some now decry these activities as liberal or socialistic and advocate their replacement with privately owned businesses. Why do we never hear an outcry for private libraries? The fact that private enterprise might be more efficient is only part of the picture because the basic motivation changes and that may not be for the better. Often, it is for the worse.

Community barn and home raisings were replaced by insurance. How often have citizens been disappointed by their trusted insurance carriers after an earthquake, hurricane, tornado or similar natural disaster? The citizens of San Francisco came together and rebuilt after the quake as did the citizens of Chicago after the fire. We came to the aid of New Orleans after Katrina. **America applauds and participates.**

Social Security is a communal effort to enhance the lives of our seniors and it has worked beautifully. Early in the last century and before, the few who outlived their working years almost always lived with and were supported by their children. That was all changed and they now lead, more or less, independent lives. You can find them in mobile home communities by the millions and in mansions worth millions. The best part is that enhancement of quality was accomplished by our national community on a pay as you go basis. What could be more basically American than that?

Medicare, on the other hand, is not on a pay as you go basis, but is really a form of welfare designed to help the elderly with the inevitable medical problems that come with age. Because of the merits of that goal, most Americans advocate Medicare in spite of the enormous tax cost. It would seem sensible, then, to change Medicare into a pay as you go program. It would satisfy America's conservative standards.

22

Chapter Seven
History

From what source and how did **American Conservative Standards** become established? They were the confluence of many systems and ideas that have been kicked around during recorded history. They are the result of painful trial and error and the stepchild of terror and atrocity. Some may have resulted from strokes of genius; but, for certain, **every last one has a historical foundation.** All human institutions, with age like all life, become imbalanced and eventually fail. **Our prime job is to remember history in order to delay failure by maintaining balance and conserving our standards.**

George Santayana said: *"Those who cannot remember the past are condemned to repeat it."* The author and a neighbor had an eMail debate concerning the possibility of freedom and democracy coming to an end in America. The author used many of the quotations found in this book to fortify history's contention that liberty is always at risk and challenged his friend to back up his opposing position with similar support. No amount of argument could sway his position – *"somehow America will muddle through"* - even though he could use no other history to substantiate his views; nor could he dispute the history cited. At the end, the friend expressed thanks for the history lesson, and declined to continue, simply saying: *"I will not change my mind."*

His beliefs are so *"in the gut"* they are no more than what he wants to believe which underlines the points made by George Bernard Shaw: *"We learn from experience that men never learn anything from experience,"* Samuel Adams: *"Mankind are governed more by their feelings than by reason,"* and George Hegel: *"What experience and history teach is this -- that people and governments never have learned anything from history, or acted on principles."*

Thomas Fuller said: *"They that buy an office must sell something,"* George F. Will said: *"Being elected to Congress is regarded as being sent on a looting raid for one's friends,"* and Andrew Jackson said: *"It is to be regretted that the rich and powerful too often bend the acts of government to their own selfish purposes."*

Is it not exactly this neighbor's kind of *"in the gut"* belief that allows politicians to obtain positions of power whereby they can satisfy the private needs of their sponsors and supporters with little regard to the strict *"General Welfare?"* Will Rogers, the humorist, said: *"If you ever injected truth into politics you have no politics."*

Who'$ Driving?

J. H. Wallis said: *"The wise and clever politician makes the passions and prejudices of his constituents one of his principal assets. Nearly all people vote not according to the best interests of the community or even according to their own best interests as decided by calm and logical reasoning, but according to their passions and prejudices."* Is it not because history is forgotten that such passions and prejudices can dominate and jeopardize liberty and democracy? When private needs become paramount; the needs of society as a whole become irrelevant and balance is lost. John Adams said: *"Remember, democracy never lasts long. It soon wastes, exhausts, and murders itself. There never was a democracy yet that did not commit suicide."*

Wiley Miller did a cartoon sequence in his "NON SEQUITUR" which illustrates this book's contention that history is forgotten thereby creating the conditions that guarantee the repetitions of history. The sequence is titled *"In Memory"* and pictures a small girl sitting on a park bench next to an elderly gentleman with a hat, glasses and reading a newspaper. The little girl comments about the strange tattoo on the man's arm which is just a series of numbers.

The old man replies that the tattoo came when he was still a child and he has not had it removed as a reminder. When the little girl asks if it is a reminder of happier days, the old man tells her the story of when the world went crazy, when political extremists blamed his people and their religion for certain terrorist acts, sent all with that particular religious belief and other political undesirables to concentration camps, and methodically murdered them. This depravity included abandoning personal names and substituting tattooed numbers on prisoner's arms.

Picture in your mind, a mal-nourished child, fenced behind chain link and barbed wire, with the Star of David sewn on her ragged dress. The old man continued that the Holocaust caused millions to die simply because of their faith. Sadly, with a tear in her eye, the little girl asked if he kept the tattoo to remind himself of the dangers of political power in extreme. **The old man said he kept it to remind her.**

Not all who were murdered in the Holocaust were Jewish. Many others who dissented were also executed including Christian theologian Dietrich Bonhoeffer who said: *"First they came for the Communists, but I was not a Communist so I did not speak out. Then they came for the Socialists and the Trade Unionists, but I was neither, so I did not speak out. Then they came for the Jews, but I was not a Jew so I did not speak out. And when they came for me, there was no one left to speak out for me."* Will you speak out now for your great grandchildren and theirs?

Who'$ Driving?

This book is a reminder. We must not forget history if our values, systems and standards are to survive. History is not only forgotten, it often can be and is distorted – there are many today who deny that the Holocaust ever happened. Those in denial have inalienable beliefs. Such *"in the gut"* beliefs give birth to terrorism, some activism, some apathy; more than likely, some birth good, however rare. *"In the gut"* religious beliefs have birthed much good, but, certainly, much evil.

It is necessary that we all recognize the greatest good for society is the only valid standard to judge human activity since it is what all want for future generations. History has demonstrated that certain objectives can only be reached communally – examples are revolution, space exploration, law and order, charity, and government *"of the people, for the people and by the people."* Special interests must be ignored. It follows that government favoring any special interests must be regarded as dangerous, tending toward imbalance. **If it is not for all the people, it is *"liberal - not narrow in bounds, opinion or judgment."***

The real authors of this book are the thinkers, strivers, statesmen, and leaders in this world who, starting well before the Age of Reason, came together over history in the interest of liberty and made our nation the greatest ever seen in this world. They are the very men who shaped and created the Conservative Standards that has made America great. Some quotes are so important, they are repeated.

History tells us that liberty is fragile and must be defended above all other values and possessions. Question the morality of your society because children of the future, like those of the past, face a grim reality with restricted liberty - a cross sewn on the dress of a forlorn little girl in a stockade could reflect unlikely, but conceivable power shifts of the future. We can't know the future, but we can be prepared. **When** *"in the gut"* **says** *"it can't happen here,"* **it is getting ever closer.**

The struggle to obtain and maintain liberty is no more than combat to limit the power of those that govern. The struggle to limit the power of those that govern is no more than combat to limit the concentration of wealth in few hands. The struggle to limit the concentration of wealth in few hands may be no more than combat to maintain a proved system of balance through taxation which spreads the wealth. Adam Smith wrote that when individuals pursue self-interest, an *"invisible hand"* would guide people to act in the public interest. The philosophical basis of capitalism, then, advocates the public interest as our societal goal.

All people have what might be called **biased and inalienable beliefs** which develop because man needs to believe. An example is the conservative belief that Corporate America is the engine that powers America. Corporations may be the infrastructure, but the real motive force lies with American consumers. Henry Ford started his company with $28,000. The billions of dollars now invested in Ford Motor came from consumers. There are neither profits nor savings without a sale. It was not until people could afford more than the base necessities that innovation and invention could find markets.

Investment capital can be created in two ways – accumulated as products from labor utilizing natural resources or saved from profits. You can have labor without capital and you can have capital working without physical labor. While labor can be made more productive through investment of capital, invention and innovation; profits and savings happen only if there is compensation for the products of labor and capital. Without compensation neither labor nor capital has potential for profit and savings. Compensation happens only when and if products are consumed.

Products sitting on shelves can and have ruined economies – it is called *"disaccumulation of capital."* Money in the pockets of consumers takes products off shelves compensating labor and capital with profits and savings allowing creation of more products – that is growth. Consumption alone creates growth, capital and wealth.

Conservatives want to believe in Corporate America so much that they overlook the lobbyists system that now exercises undo influence on our government. Power politics in Washington has reached a point that one lobbyist was just paid a $2 million bonus when he left his employer after only four years to rejoin the staff of the Representative he worked for before becoming a lobbyist. Apparently, his close connection to that powerful Representative was worth that much in anticipated benefits to the lobbyist firm and their special interest clients.

In the 1940s, 50s and 60s, there was a concentration of political power centered in the labor unions. This resulted in not conservative programs designed specifically to benefit the lower classes. The labor movement went too far, so many of our largest industries are now jeopardized by foreign competition. That does not mean that unions are bad, it means that political power became unbalanced.

A side result is that many of the upper classes fault unions to the point of blaming all our problems on union activities. Are not the size and power of labor unions limited by the size and power of the corporations with which they deal? Surely, fault lies with both! We must never forget Voltaire's: ***"Opinion has caused more trouble on this***

26

little earth than plagues or earthquakes," and Lord Acton's *"Power corrupts and absolute power corrupts absolutely."*

Adam Smith said business itself a communal activity performed by private individuals. The wealthy aristocracy and many others of the middle class think *"Laissez-faire"* capitalism justifies government policies that are pro-active business. They do not recognize that history confirms *"Laissez-faire"* only to the point where the concentration of economic power interferes with free market processes and government.

We can see such results everyday in our marketplaces. Go to the drug stores and pay a multiple of the world prices for drugs. Capitalism does not work when markets are controlled by a small number of huge corporations. Go to the grocery and buy sugar. This is not capitalism at work, it is a market manipulated by government favoring moneyed special interests. Go fill your gas tank. This is not capitalism at work, it is a market controlled by foreign cartels and corporate special interests. **Free markets work for the public benefit only if they are truly free.**

When markets are free, profits should, in theory, exceed short term interest rates by a few percentage points. Look at the basic necessities and see free competition. Look at those industries whose profits multiply short term interest rates and see markets controlled by industrial cartels. This is not free competition and does not fit the standards of our capitalistic system. Controlled markets tend to accelerate the imbalance found in the concentration of wealth.

When our economy and politics are controlled by a narrow class of the elite, democracy itself is jeopardized. It should never be forgotten that this narrow class is always transitory – their makeup changes from generation to generation. The elite tell themselves they are the best, the successful, the smartest and should run things because the common people really don't know what is best for them.

History says exactly the opposite. We have about 5,500 years of recorded history controlled almost entirely by that class. Common man painfully shed real blood, sweat and tears under their leadership. We have had only a few hundred years of widespread liberty. That is why Lord Acton told us: *"Every class is unfit to govern"* and John Adams said: *"Power always thinks it has a great soul and vast views beyond the comprehension of the weak."*

History recognizes that great political power presents a danger and our forefathers devised the *"Separation of Powers"* to protect us. Ramsey Clark erroneously said: *"A right is not what someone gives you; it's what no one can take from you."* **Rights can and have historically**

always been taken away just as all democracies have failed. We should recognize that the concentration of wealth endangers the *"Separation of Powers"* because the power politics of incumbency in imbalance defeats morality, frugality, practicality and even patriotism through the liberal misinterpretation of the *"General Welfare."*

Shifts in the concentration of wealth and power in history saw the end of enormously successful democratic societies and much progress was lost in antiquity. What could civilization be today if the liberties of the Greeks, Romans and others had not been lost? Their science, technology and medicine reached almost modern levels – steam engine (Heron,) analog computer (Antikythera,) and even brain surgery (Galen.) No one knows what else may have been lost to feudalism.

Plutarch said: *"An imbalance between rich and poor is the oldest and most fatal ailment of all republics,"* and Will and Ariel Durant said: *"Concentration of wealth is a natural result of concentration of ability, and recurs in history. The rate of concentration varies (other factors being equal) with the economic freedom permitted by morals and the law ... democracy, allowing the most liberty, accelerates it."* The concentration of wealth, then, is the inevitable result of liberty, democracy and capitalism, yet, by engendering political imbalance, is the *"oldest and most fatal ailment"* of liberty, democracy and capitalism.

This is history's most dangerous circuity.

Conservatism demands that political entities not interfere with the business world. History indicates that the business and religious worlds must not interfere with the political world.

In his Farewell Speech, Ronald Reagan said: *"We the people tell the government what to do, it doesn't tell us. We the people are the driver, the government is the car. And we decide where it should go, and by what route, and how fast."* Sir Winston Churchill said: *"However beautiful the strategy, you should occasionally look at the results."* As a society, we must maintain the moral, frugal and practical values proved by experience, and not just by theory, if we want to avoid the wrong turns of the past that returned society to feudalistic control.

There is an old science fiction story about a talking horse with great intellect. This horse, known to be a poet, devised a way to recover planets that had been ecologically ruined by man. The horse's mistress purchased our ravaged and abandoned Earth and the horse returned it to its verdant pristine beauty. While the horse became famous throughout the galaxy, no one could find any record of the horse's poetry. The horse's poetry, you see, was motion.

Who'$ Driving?

You can, I know, picture that fluid motion in your mind. The mind is a wondrous thing, and the comfort of many years comes from many sources. Humorist Will Rogers said: *"Being young is beautiful, but being old is comfortable."* What was once liberal became conservative because it proved comfortable. Mankind is yet young, but we have reached some precious comforts found in the conservative standards all Americans hold highest.

Aristotle said: *"The most perfect political community is one in which the middle class is in control, and outnumbers both of the other classes."* We may have had this balance when America was primarily rural and the numerous farmers were the middle class. With urbanization, however, the balance may have been lost following the Civil War and then regained over the period following the Great Depression. Are we in danger of losing it again? Those men and women quoted in this book say it almost certainly will be lost again.

Wisdom In-Stalled

Participation sports are life in small scale
They show what we are: be it strong, be it frail
We compete on our own or as part of a team
Playing by the rules essential to the scheme
Just as it is in life, to lose is not to fail
An opportunity to try again for the chance to prevail
Golf, the most difficult game man has devised
The wayward are lost; can be harshly penalized
You can cheat or you can play it on the square
You answer only to yourself, as in life, so beware
The temptation to cheat is great, but really a lie
You can't like yourself much if you cheat to get by
In golf as in life, most, if any, don't really know how
Even after years of unspoken fears, most will avow
To improve and not cheat at least once ere they die
Frustrated by golf, not sure of the what or even the why
It is the same for us all, written in prose or in poem
This microcosm of life, the lesson really came home
Played nine, and then off to the men's room for needed relief
Got more, for the moral of this poem became my belief
From the next stall, a golfer said – and he did not lie
"For the first time today, I know what I am doing and why!"

Who'$ Driving?

The American people have been smothered by propaganda concerning *"Laissez-faire"* to the point that we may no longer know exactly what we are doing or why. Arnold Toynbee said about *"Laissez-faire"* capitalism: ***"it came to be believed in as a gospel, [...] from which it was regarded as little short of immoral to depart."*** *"Laissez-faire"* is not gospel and it must be a two way street.

Government must lay down certain guidelines for business to protect the public from fraud and monopolies, and enforce socially accepted employment practices. Grover Cleveland said: ***"He mocks the people who proposes that the government shall protect the rich and that they in turn will care for the laboring poor."*** The concentration of wealth in totalitarian nations confirms history's lesson that the rich will hoard all they can. It is part of the natural processes of humanity. They are just doing something our system values highly. The problem is not the wealth; it is *"an imbalance between the rich and poor."*

In his farewell speech, Ronald Reagan said: *"An informed patriotism is what we want. And are we doing a good enough job teaching our children what America is and what she represents in the long history of the world? Those of us who are over thirty-five or so years of age grew up in a different America. We were taught, very directly, what it means to be an American. And we absorbed, almost in the air, a love of country and an appreciation of its institutions. If you didn't get these things from your family, you got them from the neighborhood, from the father down the street who fought in Korea of the family who lost someone at Anzio. Or you could get a sense of patriotism from school. And if all else failed, you could get a sense of patriotism from the popular culture. The movies celebrated democratic values and implicitly reinforced the idea that America was special."*

The Great Communicator knew America is about the children. America is not about corporations; it is about personal endeavor and success, but mostly America is about the children. **Our present government is neither frugal nor practical - there is little balance in huge trade deficits and the National Debt.** For these reasons our government is not moral, and it simply does not understand that America is about the children and the future. Must we not also question even its patriotism since enormous multi-national corporations have its ear?

For the children of the future, we must make sure that *"being young"* remains *"beautiful."* No special interest should be able to buy favoritism from any level of government. Who's driving?

Chapter Eight
What we are

In America, we have an untenable situation where conservatives and liberals are at odds and have little, if any, dialog. Part of that, if not most, stems from a changing definition of what it means to be *"liberal or conservative"* and part stems from our diversity. Much, also, stems from tendentious beliefs so ingrained that even historic converse evidence is discarded as unworthy. **Since the definitions of conservative and liberal are blurred; this book necessarily resorts to made-up words -** an exercise in futility underlining that current labels have little meaning.

Rep. Carl Albert said: *"I very much dislike doctrinaire liberals -- they want to own your minds. And I don't like reactionary conservatives. I like to face issues in terms of conditions and not in terms of someone's inborn political philosophy."*

Many liberals use the pejorative term *"neofeudalism"* to smear conservatives. They observe that government programs have the effect of accelerating the concentration of wealth in the hands of a few thereby increasing the political power of the rich and decreasing the power of the poor. Some equate the net effect to classic feudalism – power and control from the top down the social hierarchy. Conservatives use the pejorative term *"liberal"* to malign any disagreement.

Voltaire said: ***"In general, the art of government consists of taking as much money as possible from one party of the citizens to give to the other."*** Americans want our government *"of the people, by the people, and for the people"* to contradict Voltaire. Americans want to defend conservative standards so that our government *"shall not perish from the earth,"* and also want to make sure that government activities satisfy the *"General Welfare"* of *"all the people."*

Private enterprise may run a more efficient police force, but what happens when an immoral person gains control of the private police force? Can that happen? History holds no doubt. It has often happened in publicly controlled police departments. The only effective control for corruption, public or private, is the ballot box.

The ballot box is the ultimate power and it must prevail. In order to insure the power of the ballot box, we must defend our most basic conservative standards. Power and control must come from all levels of the social hierarchy. This book is essentially concerned with how America can defend the standards and values that have made this nation the greatest in history using the arguments and observations of the great people that helped create our systems, standards and values. Virtually all Americans believe that all human activity is best performed by individuals pursuing their own self interest and that government is a necessary evil. **We tolerate government to insure a balanced and level playing field.**

Why do we need made-up words? Anna Quindlen compendiously wrote in Newsweek: *"Call it realignment or moderation. Just don't call it liberal or conservative, Democratic or Republican. Those labels really don't apply."* Politically, conservatives are mostly Republicans; many are religious traditionalists; most support "Laissez-faire" and Corporate America almost to the point of worship; and applaud the actions of their leadership without question. Politically, liberals are usually Democrats; quite a few support environmental activisms; most are pro-labor and the working classes; some advocate communal health programs; and applaud the actions of their leadership without question.

The problem arises when you try to apply the strict definitions of liberal and conservative. If the two sides are ever going to work together, we first need to understand what we are. Consider the list of America's conservative standards on Page 15. Recognize that it is a given. There can be no doubt that these are the standards that virtually all Americans want to conserve – in these, **all Americans are conservative.**

In Chapter 22, you will find an argument concerning pollution. It is not about global warming which may or may not have validity. It is about our children who have utmost validity. Most likely, virtually all Americans will support this argument. **Are we then all liberal?**

Henry Kissinger said concerning our allies: *"Confidence in America is an important element for worldwide order."* When the majority of your allies advise you against a contemplated action, disregarding their advice will damage their confidence and must be regarded as **reckless.** To then ridicule them for forgetting our history, forgets world history. Without America, the French might speak German. Without France, Americans most likely would sing *"God save the Queen."*

We have conservative political leaders who are liberals in their reckless spending and foreign policies. We have liberal political leaders who conservatively oppose reckless spending and foreign policy. We have both conservative and liberal leaders and political pundits advocating policies historically proved to endanger liberty. We have conservatives and liberals unwilling to listen, discuss or consider history.

Powerful political leaders of both political parties favor pro-active government programs favoring special interests. Such programs are by nature *"liberal - not narrow in bounds, opinion or judgment"* as defined by America's conservative standards. Such leaders, on right and left, are **not conservative** and, in this book, termed **"Nonservative."**

Also, you will find the pejorative labels: *"CosCons"* and *"LamLibs,"* which terms are used to distinguish these vocal minorities from the much greater number of American moderates. You may be a CosCon or Lam Lib if your opinions and political positions are just *"in the gut"* knowing you are right. Both sides' final defense is: *"I'm not going to change my mind."* That cop out confirms their status.

CosCons are *"cosmetic conservatives"* so termed as they have forgotten history and choose a political party favoring pro-active government for special interests (business or religious) failing to recognize that democracy must always be *"for the people."* The special interests they oppose include the adult poor and disadvantaged, the labor movement, and those advocating government supports for any communal activities that may interfere with private enterprise.

LamLibs are *"lamina liberals"* so termed as they have forgotten history and choose a political party favoring pro-active government for special interests (workers and disadvantaged) failing to recognize that inequities are essential to a capitalist system. The special interests they oppose include the rich and powerful, corporate America and those advocating government supports for specific private endeavors.

RAP are the rich and powerful - this is not a derogation of wealth. Wealth is the essential motivating goal that makes our capitalistic system work. This book is distrustful of RAP power because that power is often used to satisfy only their private interests. Leadership is essential, but the private interests of leaders can overwhelm the *"General Welfare"* of the people – as illustrated by the history that ended all democracies!

Proservatives support and defend the conservative standards defined in Chapter Four. While conservative, they are also realistically progressive, usually believing in the merits of national defense, public schooling, police, emergency services, Medicare and Social Security. They accept that some human activities are best done communally in the interest of the narrow interpretation of the *"General Welfare."* Although they probably are not aware of critical history, they want all of the children to have a balanced and level playing field

Proservatives want government to stay out of their lives as much as possible, but they are willing to carry their fair share of necessary and important government. In times of crisis, they will shoulder arms. At all times, they want what is best for America and especially for the children. *"We the people"* are mostly Proservatives.

The general population is not a special interest in any of its phases – youth, adult and the aged. Government programs pro-active all citizens of any age group are neither liberal nor socialistic. It is conservative to care for our own – it is government *"of all the people, by all the people and for all the people."* We cannot stand for long an elastic Constitution so the *"General Welfare"* **clause must have limitations!**

All conservatives are not CosCons just as all liberals are not LamLibs. **It is a matter of degree, but it is more a matter of attitude.** It is just how solidified are the *"in the gut"* beliefs. It is a predisposition to reject any and all contrary opinions combined with an unyielding sense of perfection – an overly typical American fault.

As a CosCon, you are unwilling to question. You are a conservative fully backing your Republican leadership. You know *"in your gut"* that your position is the only reasonable one and you are *"not going to change your mind."* You know that Corporate America is the engine that powers America and you back it without question. You know that we are doing the right thing trying to bring democracy to Iraq. But, America, because of the liberals, is not on the right track in your eyes.

As a LamLib, you are unwilling to question. You are a liberal fully backing your Democratic leadership. You know *"in your gut"* that your position is the only reasonable one and you are *"not going to change your mind."* You know that the little people in America are getting the short end of the stick. You know that we are not doing the right thing trying to bring democracy to Iraq. Because of the conservatives, America is not on the right track in your eyes, and you feel more Federal programs are needed to alleviate the problems of our lowest classes.

Whether on right or left, should we not all focus on and bring to an end the reckless fiscal policies and programs of our elastic government? Are you happy with the deficit and the enormous trade imbalance? Must we not recognize that our Constitutional protections have been significantly altered by past Court decisions? Must we not be acutely aware that our Constitution can be suspended at some time in the future?

The hard-nosed party believers will answer differently than the vast majority of Americans because they know, *"in their gut,"* that they are right. Which begs the question: is the author right? He believes he has a solid foundation from history and those quoted in this book. If you disagree, make sure you have solid foundation in history, because history created our standards and has an undeniable propensity for repetition.

Chapter Nine
Lesson

Dwight Eisenhower (1890-1969)

Eisenhower in his "Farewell Speech (1961) warned us: *"In the councils of government, we must guard against the acquisition of unwarranted influence, whether sought or unsought, by the military industrial complex. The potential for the disastrous rise of misplaced power exists and will persist. We must never let the weight of this combination endanger our liberties or democratic processes. We should take nothing for granted."*

John F. Kennedy (1917-1963)

John F. Kennedy said: *"... ask not what your country can do for you—ask what you can do for your country."* and we all listened. The dangers observed in our system stem from those unique corporate immortals who do not simply ask what the country can do for them; they demand that the country do whatever it is they want. They back up those demands with the monetary gifts our Nonservative politicians need to be and stay elected.

Our Founding Fathers had at least three great fears: powerful government, religious discrimination and corporations. The battle of ideologies between the Federalists (elitists) and the Republican-Democrats (populists) was fought out and won by the latter over 200 years ago when Thomas Jefferson and James Madison achieved almost all they wanted in our Bill of Rights. It is unfortunate that, they failed to get an Amendment restraining the power of corporations which both repeatedly stated was of paramount importance.

The conflict between elitists and populists in the United States now has come down to a battle between the Republican Nonservatives allied with the CosCons against the Democrat Nonservatives aligned with LamLibs. It is time for all to set aside our prideful differences, get back to basics and focus on our most basic conservative values.

Lord Acton (1834-1902)

Famed historian John Emerich Edward Dalberg-Acton, 1st Baron Acton, issued sharp warnings that political power is the most serious threat to liberty. Acton's existing writings are full of notable insights. He wrote: *"Liberty is not a means to a higher political end. It is itself the highest political end...liberty is the only object which benefits all alike, and provokes no sincere opposition...The danger is not that a particular class is unfit to govern. Every class is unfit to govern...Power tends to corrupt, and absolute power corrupts absolutely."*

It is safe to observe that his once liberal ideas are now among our most cherished conservative ideals.

Our Founding Fathers foresaw a potential danger in the concentration of wealth in few hands and that unbalanced condition may be here now. While stock ownership may be widespread, the control of these humongous, immortal corporations (*"persons"* in the eyes of the law) and, perhaps, our government rests solidly in the hands of our managerial aristocracy.

How humongous is humongous? The gross domestic product of Sweden (population over 9 million) is less than the annual sales of Wal-Mart. Wal-Mart is, at its very core, merely a piece of paper. In 2001, only forty-seven of the one hundred world's largest economies were nations and fifty-three were corporations. Add up the annual budgets of all the political entities in the United States – federal, state, cities, counties, etc. Their total equals about two-thirds (66.6%) of the combined revenues of just fifty of our largest corporations.

Who'$ Driving?

The first corporations in America were the colonies themselves, chartered by the British crown. Thomas Jefferson wanted to include *"freedom from monopolies"* in the Bill of Rights. Jefferson referred to corporations often as monopolies since most corporations of his time and experience were just that. While unsuccessful in that proposal, he did later write, *"I hope that we shall crush in its birth the aristocracy of our moneyed corporations, which dare already to challenge our government to a trial of strength, and bid defiance to the laws of our country."*

We have, without doubt, the greatest political system ever devised on this earth. It is the legacy of liberty. Any institution that threatens liberty jeopardizes our basic political system. These corporate *"persons"* are immortal and have all the legal rights of American citizens other than the right to vote; yet, with neither soul nor conscience, they pose a threat to our basic political system. That threat is the corruption that stems from unbalanced financial and political power.

Niccolo Machiavelli (1469-1527)

The threat of corruption is reminiscent of Machiavelli. According to Lord Acton, Machiavelli *"was an acute politician, sincerely anxious that the obstacles to the intelligent government of Italy should be swept away. It appeared to him that the most vexatious obstacle to intellect is conscience, and that the vigorous use of statecraft necessary for the success of difficult schemes would never be made if governments allowed themselves to be hampered by the precepts of the copy-book.*

*"His audacious doctrine was avowed in the succeeding age, by men whose personal character otherwise stood high. They saw that in critical times good men have seldom strength for their goodness, and yield to those who have grasped the meaning of the maxim that you cannot make an omelet if you are afraid to break the eggs. They saw that public morality differs from private, because no government can turn the other cheek, or can admit that mercy is better than justice. **And they could not define the difference, or draw the limits of exception; or tell what other standard for a nation's acts there is than the judgment which heaven pronounces in this world by success."***

Who'$ Driving?

Most people judge corporations to be *"good"* simply because they are successful. That men should understand that corporations do not exist by divine right is reason enough to bind them to some higher standard than *"success."* Other than success, there are presently no other moral judgments as to their existence; and, certainly, there should be just as there are judgments for everything else man has created.

The list of important men of history who acknowledged a fear of corporations is long and laden with honors: Adam Smith, Thomas Jefferson, James Madison, Andrew Jackson, Abraham Lincoln, Theodore Roosevelt and Dwight Eisenhower to name a few.

Feudalism is a system whereby serf workers were supervised by vassals for the prime benefit of overlords and the aristocracy. Huge corporations, with their large, secured, fortress buildings have many workers supervised by management for the prime benefit of the corporate aristocracy and invisible stockholders. Is there a great difference?

Corporations are the only *"persons"* that cannot be tried in criminal court. If a corporation is a *"person,"* why can't there be prosecution? Doesn't the phrase *"corporations are the only persons"* sound oxymoronic? Or, is it simply just dumb?

Lesson

We've heard it said many times
"Young and dumb," that is doubtless
Now, as my hair grays
I know it's redundant, certainly
These two words are synonymous
As I grow older, my wisdom grows too
Now I offer a gift of that wisdom for you
It is the wisest thing I've ever said
Old and dumb are synonyms too

Sageisms:

"Trickle-down theory. The less than elegant metaphor that if one feeds the horse enough oats, some will pass through to the road for the sparrows." -John Kenneth Galbraith

"Few men have virtue enough to withstand the highest bidder."
-George Washington

Chapter Ten
Neither soul nor conscience

Within all large corporations, control should be a balance of power among shareholders, boards and top executives. The board is supposed to be an agent for the stockholders protecting their interests, but there may be little incentive to do that. The stockholder base is widely dispersed and individual stockholders rarely monitor and usually vote passively. The board, then, looks to hired management for direction.

Management has enormous incentive to influence the board in ways that may not be in the best interest of stockholders. The *"arrogance of officialdom"* is found in corporate as well as political fields. Corporate managerial insiders often have seats on the board and usually the chair. One of the board's chief responsibilities is hiring and firing top level management, determining compensation, bonus levels and retirement compensation. **This is a built-in conflict of interest.**

Stock options further the conflict of interest. If the stock advances in value, the officers gain greater rewards, but now have incentive to overstate results and not book expenses such as stock options. Large institutional investors are trying to more closely monitor corporate boards and management. It is doubtful if they are looking into the ethics of corporate management and their interaction with government. These are the areas of interest to the voters. Who's driving the corporations?

When corporations are controlled by management rather than the board or the stockholders, there is dangerous imbalance. Hypothetically, an individual runs a corporation for some time, but the business has not been doing as well as desired. A large stockholder finally pressures the CEO to resign so improvement is possible. Stockholders are encouraged until they discover that the outgoing CEO will be paid his $2.5 million salary for the next five years.

That is just the deal Phillip B. Rooney received when terminated as CEO of WMX Technologies Inc in 1997. The board acquiesced based on their interpretation of his contract. Who exactly is writing contracts like this and why? Who is looking out for the stockholders?

Favorable contracts written by corporate employees for other employees are not in the interests of stockholders. Executives leaving for any reason – fired, retired, downsized, merged out and quitting – are unreasonably compensated. Huge rewards even when they have failed.

Hypothetically an individual running a very large corporation brings in an outsider to invigorate the business. After a few months, something happens to damage the relationship between the two, and the new guy is relieved of his duties. This is a situation that probably happens often. To obtain his services in the first place, he was given a favorable contract. This sounds normal, but at these levels nothing is normal.

Michael Ovitz was hired by Michael Eisner at Disney. For his 14 month disappointing tenure, he received an exit package estimated around $90 million. Stockholders justifiably objected.

Stephen Hilbert left Conseco under pressure with a $70 million exit package. The company eventually bankrupted so he may have lost some of these benefits. Years later, the company sued him for unpaid loans of $250 million. Why are corporations lending executives such outrageous sums? Since his departure, three other CEOs have come and gone with large exit packages.

Such outrageous incidents can happen only because corporations have become so enormous that these dollar amounts are small in relation to the overall numbers and because management controls the board and is insulated from stockholders. Management will write generous contracts and they get the same – it is not their money being thrown liberally around.

Lord Acton words: *"The danger is not that a particular class is unfit to govern. Every class is unfit to govern...Power tends to corrupt, and absolute power corrupts absolutely"* can apply to the world of corporate America as well as the world of politics.

Many boards and senior management follow ethical standards, but not all. Corporations need a system of checks and balances with full open disclosure and whistle-blower protection to stop unethical behavior, intentional or otherwise. Hypothetically, a top level committee decides to increase profits through budget cuts. Memos go out and lower-level managers decide to postpone certain needed safety upgrades to achieve the ordered cuts. Multiple levels of power negate conscience and ethics.

In 2005, a BP oil refinery in Texas City explodes killing 15 and injuring 170 employees because management ignored documented requests for safety modifications, so as to implement budget cuts. Why are that management and board not prosecuted for negligent homicide? In huge size, every responsible person points at others. This company earned over $6 billion in 2006. Were these budget cuts moral?

Americans wants capitalism to be conserved. Huge corporations should be feared as they cause imbalance by limiting competition and by accelerating the concentration of wealth. At the very least, we must take corporations out of the political arena. Who's driving?

Chapter Eleven
Three Great Fears

Arnold Toynbee said: *"It is a great law of social development that the movement from slavery to freedom is also a movement from security to insecurity of maintenance."* Feudal systems were, by nature, unbalanced and could only be maintained by force. Liberty requires freedom from force so that security is sacrificed. Democracy requires a delicate balance for maintenance.

The Articles of Confederation were adopted by the states in 1781. America's *"experiment"* (de Tocqueville) with democracy had begun. While it was replaced by our current Constitution, little remembered is that there was a great struggle between two competing camps of thought: The Federalist Party and the Democratic-Republican Party.

The Democratic-Republican Party – the modern Democratic Party of today – was originally known as the *"Republican Party."* Historians now use the combination to distinguish it from the Republican Party that was established in 1854 combining three other political parties.

Thomas Jefferson (1743-1826)

Thomas Jefferson and James Madison of the Republican Party advocated limited government to be elected and controlled by the general populous. This contrasted to the Federalists who advocated a strong government. Democratic-Republicans dominated the elections of both 1800 and 1804 effectively ending the Federalists as a political party.

In a land of farmers, it is hard to imagine that our founding fathers could conceive of the enormous commercial empire that has since swept over our nation. Madison called agriculture *"the great staple of America."* He wrote: *"The class of citizens, who provide at once their own food and their own raiment, may be viewed as the most truly independent and happy. They are more: they are the best basis of public liberty, and the strongest bulwark of public safety. It follows, that the greater the proportion of this class to the whole society, the more free, the more independent, and the more happy must be the society itself."* We can now say much of the same about the American middle class Proservatives except few farm and none spin and sew.

James Madison (1751-1836)

A bank was among the first privately-owned corporations and was highly controversial especially when the bank got involved in politics, so there were several attempts to terminate its charter. Like virtually all corporations, the bank eventually failed in 1841. In a letter James Madison said: *"With regard to Banks, they have taken too deep and too wide a root in social transactions, to be got rid of altogether, if that were desirable. ...they have a hold on public opinion, which alone would make it expedient to aim rather at the improvement, than the suppression of them. As now generally constituted, their advantages whatever they be, are outweighed by the excesses of their paper emissions, and the partialities and corruption with which they are administered."*

John Locke (1632-1704)

While Madison distrusted letting companies have great power, he was at the time more concerned with the concept of *"natural rights,"* which was the central theme of the Revolutionary era generation inspired by the writings of John Locke. Madison was acutely aware of the danger in the rise of corporate power late in his career, but they may not have been obvious to him when he helped write the Constitution. The full implications of industrial revolution were, apparently, also not Jefferson's primary concern.

The Second Treatise on Government (1698,) by John Locke defined the *"natural rights"* that all people inherit to by virtue of their common humanity. He wrote: *"All men by nature are equal...in that equal right that every man hath to his natural freedom, without being subjected to the will or authority of any other man; ... being all equal and independent, no one ought to harm another in his life, health, liberty or possessions..."*

In Jefferson's *"Summary View of the Rights of British America"* (1774) he wrote about this *"natural right:"* *"The God who gave us life, gave us liberty at the same time: the hand of force may destroy, but cannot disjoin them."* His first draft of the Declaration of Independence declared: *"We hold these truths to be sacred and undeniable; that all men are created equal and independent, that from that equal creation they derive rights inherent and unalienable, among which are the preservation of life, and liberty, and the pursuit of happiness."* The natural rights come in the form of a representative government protective from those forces that previously had dominated, enslaved and taken advantage – foreign government and feudal corporations.

Alexander Hamilton, on the other hand, was concerned with the danger of people having full *"natural rights."* He warned of the risks in such idealism in the Federalist Papers: *"Reflections of this kind may have trifling weight with men [like you] who hope to see realized in America the halcyon scenes of the poetic or fabulous age; but to those [among us Federalists] who believe we are likely to experience a common portion of the vicissitudes and calamities which have fallen to the lot of other nations, they must appear entitled to serious attention. Such men [as those of us who would lead this nation] must behold the actual situation of their country with painful solicitude, and depreciate the evils which ambition or revenge might, with too much facility, inflict upon it."*

Jefferson and Madison feared the concentration of wealth and that the government, imitating France, would take for itself our *"natural rights."* Hamilton, Adams and the Federalists feared the crowd would combine to use their political power to take private property from the wealthy as also had been seen in the French Revolution. The first ten amendments (the Bill of Rights) to the Constitution were designed to prevent either from happening.

Jefferson's view that people come first and institutions second is reflected in his well document view of the *"three threats"* to human natural rights. The three threats were: strong governments, organized religions and commercial monopolies. These institutions must be subordinate to the *"natural rights"* of humans.

The fear of governments was fear of the elitism and power of feudal kingdoms. The Federalists generally accepted the Calvinist notion that wealth was a sign of a blessing from above and involved a built-in morality – a concept contradicted by Machiavelli's *"audacious doctrine."* They were wary of the common person. Because the Senate was comprised mainly of wealthy men, mostly Federalist, the Democratic-Republicans opposed state legislatures appointing Senators. It was not until the ratification of the 17th Amendment in 1913 that the Senate was elected by the public.

Jefferson wrote to Adams: *"The artificial aristocracy is a mischievous ingredient in government, and provision should be made to prevent its ascendancy. On the question, what is the best provision, you and I differ; but we differ as rational friends, using the free exercise of our own reason, and mutually indulging its errors. You think it best to put the pseudo-aristoi into a separate chamber of legislation [the Senate], where they may be hindered from doing mischief by their coordinate branches, and where, also, they may be a protection to wealth against the agrarian and plundering enterprises of the majority of the people.* **I think that to give them power in order to prevent them from doing mischief, is arming them for it, and increasing instead of remedying the evil."**

Commercial monopolies (overly powerful corporations) and the *"pseudo aristoi"* of very wealthy persons Jefferson viewed as a prime threat. There are many examples in his writings where he advocated that control of corporations be written into the Bill of Rights. Both he and Madison were disappointed that the Constitution did not specifically curtail the potential rise of commercial monopolies like the East India Company. They both felt that *"freedom against monopolies"* is a basic right. Jefferson's fear anticipated the rise of our corporate aristocracy and the imbalance threatening our basic standards now.

Almost all of Thomas Jefferson's visions for our Bill of Rights except *"freedom from monopolies in commerce."* were adopted. Led by Adams, the Federalists kept that provision out. The result can be seen in the inordinate power wielded by immense corporations today.

While many argue that these corporations are responsible for our prosperity, their part might just as well have happened under individual entrepreneurs or partnerships without the use of artificial *"persons."* It most likely would have. This is another argument that cannot be settled.

We look back on history and rejoice that Jefferson and Madison won out over the Federalists on most issues. Now we need to regret that they lost this particular battle. After all, corporations are creations of humans and they should serve and not dominate their creators.

In time Jefferson's warning gained weight from actual experience and the Sherman Antitrust Act of 1890 tried to rectify this inadequacy. Now its enforcement is the hands of bureaucrats heavily influenced by corporate lobbyists. Whenever the government protects or favors one business competitor over another or all others, we have the kind of imbalance that led to the rebellion in Boston.

We revere the *"Boston Tea Party"* and those that risked their lives as one of the great events in our history because corporate favoritism is an abomination, jeopardizing the will of the people by limiting their freedom of choice. Samuel Webster said: *"Let monopolies and all kinds and degrees of oppression be carefully guarded against."*

Andrew Jackson said: *"Every man is equally entitled to protection by law; but when the laws undertake to add...artificial distinctions, to grant titles, gratuities, and exclusive privileges, to make the rich richer and the potent more powerful, the humble members of society – the farmers, mechanics, and laborers – who have neither the time nor the means of securing like favors to themselves, have a right to complain of the injustice of their government."*

How is it that our CosCon element supports a party that favors big government and big spending to benefit the corporate aristocracy? How is it that our LamLib contingent cannot recognize the futility of throwing money at social problems? It is moronic!

How is it that we have reached a situation where our two parties are becoming one in similarity? Have we reverted back to Jefferson's Democratic-Republican Party? Or, is it just that they are both so greatly under the influences of our corporate aristocracy's lobbyists that they really have become similar and Nonservative? By becoming similar, the danger of powerful government is increased. It is moronic!

How is it that we have reached a situation where right-wing Christian traditionalists are working for a Christian unity so as to wield greater political power? This could compromise the wall between church and state. It is moronic!

How is it that we have reached a situation where writings on paper (corporate charters) provide *"inherent and unalienable"* rights to artificial entities? It is moronic!

The Three Fears are back and that is moronic!

Who'$ Driving?

Lord Acton admired America in that liberty is more secure here than almost anywhere. He wrote: *"liberty depends on the division of power. Democracy tends to the unity of power ... Federalism is the one possible check upon concentration and centralism."* Federalism demands a more conservative interpretation of the *"General Welfare"* clause to limit the influence of private interests. America needs to make a new beginning based on old standards.

Blossoms

Fresh beginnings in every day
Blossoms fragrant along the way
Many enjoyments, certainly pain
Both are part of our joyous refrain.
Treat pain with courage and good sense
Knowing with calm self-confidence
Tomorrow will bring a new refrain
Smell the flowers, begin again

Sageisms:

"Educate and inform the whole mass of the people.... They are the only sure reliance for the preservation of our liberty." -Thomas Jefferson

"The first duty of government is to see that people have food, fuel, and clothes. The second, that they have means of moral and intellectual education." -John Ruskin

"So potent was religion in persuading to evil deeds." —Lucretius

"Both political parties have their good times and bad times, only they have them at different times." -Will Rogers

"Injustice anywhere is a threat to justice everywhere."
-Martin Luther King Jr.

"When there is a lack of honor in government, the morals of the whole people are poisoned." -Herbert Hoover

Chapter Twelve
Corporate History

CosCons want to return to *"Laissez-faire"* – the total absence of government interference in business and industry. They think, with solid justification, that free competition is the best path for progress. But, they seem to want to return control of the political world back to the *"elitist"* RAP because they are supposedly the ones who provide the investment that creates jobs. They are wrong. The consumer, responding to innovation and invention, provided the enormous investment that is the Corporate America of today. Bill Gates earned his billions from consumers; he did not simply invest billions.

Virtually all Americans believe in *"Laissez-faire"* and free enterprise, as we should. There is, however, a built in danger that requires regulation to avoid because free enterprise requires a level playing field that is not found in real life. The result is that some competitors will be more successful than others, sometimes simply because of the vagaries of location. Danger lurks when the more successful can buy out their weaker competition or use unfair pricing practices to drive the less capable out of business and discourage new competition. There is little doubt that passive pricing collusion among large corporations is common – it is the expected result of imbalance.

Karl Marx observed this process and predicted dire consequences leading to a classless society. He was terribly mistaken and caused a lot of misery through his followers (the religious and philosophical beliefs of the elite have historically caused many of common man's problems.) But his observation that wealth and power tended to concentrate in fewer and fewer hands was and is correct. We see it every day as corporate giants buy out other corporate giants. These immortals grow mostly through acquisition and only sometimes through innovation. Democracy may in time (and perhaps already has) become plutocracy and the latter, by its very nature, is corrupting.

Older citizens can confirm the expansion of Corporate America from their own experience. In the first half of the last century, virtually every business in every town was locally owned and operated. From the grocery stores to the banks to the gas stations, almost all were single store operations. Now, most business is done by branches of huge corporations or by franchises. To be sure, there are an enormous number of smaller, privately owned businesses – which is what free enterprise is really about. These people, however, have very little influence in the political world; which is also true of the legions of middle and lower management and factory workers in big industry.

The classic example of the danger of consolidation is the Standard Oil monopoly, which bought up their competition and used cutthroat pricing on a regional basis to drive others out of business. Eventually Standard Oil controlled much of the entire oil industry in America and was able to control markets and that made the Rockefellers one of the richest families in the world. It was so unfair, that the Government finally used anti-trust laws to break up Standard Oil. In recent years, these corporations have pretty much been rejoined and the result is an oil cartel dominated by a few giant players.

John D. Rockefeller (1839-1937)

That is not to say that there is inherent evil in any monopoly. The patent laws justly protect inventors from competitors. Public utilities are by their very nature, legal monopolies. But, they have to be regulated. Many large corporations attained their size by outperforming competition and are run by honorable men, but not all.

In the 1920's, some of the rich and powerful bought public utilities up under the guise that private enterprise could do it better. It was the collapse of the frenzied speculative bubble accompanying this privatization that actually triggered the stock market collapse in 1929

Without regulation, we would be forced to pay exorbitant prices like we now pay for drugs and oil. When the government abandons enforcement of the anti-trust laws and fair business practice laws, a dangerous, unbalanced economic environment is the result.

Corporations are legal *"persons,"* **superior to human citizen in rights, privileges and influence.** Corporations cannot cast ballots, but they can vote with dollars. Votes are cheap, dollars are dear. In the 2000-election, corporations contributed $696 million to candidates for federal office. In the world there are only a few democracies where such donations are allowed. The Supreme Court affirmed the right of corporations to make such campaign contributions in a 1978 case.

Who'$ Driving?

Corporations made their first appearance in the 17th-century in Europe. Originally, they were chartered only for a specific public mission and authorized to exist for a specific length of time. One example: the Massachusetts Bay Company was chartered by King Charles I in 1628 to help settle the new colonies in America.

By pooling capital from many investors (a communal activity,) corporations were able to launch ambitious ventures. It was anticipated that these ventures would expand the wealth and power of the government. Not only would they provide the sources of raw materials, they would provide markets for manufactured and other exported goods. A corporation was simply a feudal (an inheritable property) structure designed to extend the control of the government; no more, no less.

Men and women were persuaded to make the move to the New World by corporate promoters. Convicts were offered the opportunity to migrate to the colonies instead of serving time in prison. Most colonists could not themselves pay the cost of passage. Ships' captains received cash rewards to secure indenture contracts from migrants. These indentured workers often heard grandiose promises or might even be kidnapped since the corporations needed to fill their ships.

Indentured workers *"agreed"* to work for a specified number of years, then were freed and paid *"freedom dues"* which could include a tract of land. Even some African ancestry settlers were released under the indenture program, although after 1660 life long slavery, sadly, became the rule enforced by feudal corporations.

Our Founding Fathers had close memories from parents and grandparents of the brutality used to enforce indenture agreements and the *"press gangs"* used to find *"recruits."* Enforcement and exploitation by the feudal corporate settlement companies violated basic human rights. Today, many of the basic aspects that made feudalism work in the middle ages would be regarded as extortion or slavery.

As a result, radical notions of *"unalienable rights"* to *"life, liberty and the pursuit of happiness"* inspired our Founding Fathers to revolution. The fight was not only to gain independence from British rule; it was to also break away from and end the brutality of the feudal corporations chartered by the Crown that were exploiting our wealth and dominating our trade. The British East India Company had a monopoly of Eastern trade by charter and the Boston Tea Party was a protest against that monopoly.

Our forefathers had a deep seated fear of corporations. They wisely instituted legal controls to limit corporations to public benefit purposes only, such as road and canal construction in response to the profit potential. Following a precedent used in Britain, legislation expressly forbade any attempts by corporations to involve themselves in elections or public and civic policies. All charters had specific life terms and could be revoked if laws were broken or if assets were spent to influence law-making or elections.

The chartered purpose was the only legal activity. The only property that could be owned had to be essential to the corporate purpose and could not be stock in other corporations. If a corporation exceeded its authority or caused public harm, its charter was revoked. Owners and managers were held responsible for any criminal activity. During the first 100 years following our Revolution, the corporate chartering process was closely monitored by state governing bodies so few charters were authorized and those were debated publicly. State constitutions and laws closely monitored the conditions of operation and management activities were closely defined.

All corporate charters had a set time limit after which the corporation had to be liquidated and its assets distributed to the stockholders. The amount of capitalization, issuance of debt instruments and property purchased were strictly limited. Often, even the amount of profits was legislated. All accounting records were subject to legislative scrutiny. No corporation could buy another corporation.

It was common for the voting rights of large stockholders to be limited by a process called scale voting. Interlocking directorates were illegal and directors could be removed at the will of shareholders. The limited liability of directors and stockholders, that is now universal, was illegal. Any violation of law or corporate charter limits was punished by dissolution.

Eventually, American manufacturers formed corporations (for estate purposes) to create private wealth with no public mission contemplated. This created a legal problem: how to treat corporations under the law. The long running Marshall Supreme Court created a national market by declaring as unconstitutional the trade barriers legislated by the states; and by invoking the Constitution's *"obligation of contracts" clause* (Article 1, Section 10), which states that *"no state shall...pass any...law impairing the obligation of contracts."*

As time passed, corporations began to ignore these limitations and our legislators turned a well compensated blind eye. Conglomerates and trusts were becoming common so management could influence politics and control natural resources and the labor force. Company towns arose, labor organizers were blacklisted, and private armies kept workers subdued as corporate control went to absentee owners rather than being community based. The concentration of corporate wealth was underway.

The RAP began a propaganda program to convince voters that legislatures were wasting time and money supervising the corporations. Then, as now, they appealed to the philosophical basis of *"Laissez-faire"* capitalism. With their enormous wealth, they were able to corrupt the politicians – then, as now - by sending paid *"borers"* to the capitol buildings to lobby for their interests.

The Civil War gave rise to copious pork barrel benefits and the RAP used the profits to lobby for and gain limited liability, extended charter durations and circumvented the close public supervision. The court benches (seated by lawyers who gained prominence representing the violating corporations) aided this process, reinterpreting the U.S. Constitution. They were able to do this because the passage of time had virtually wiped out the memory of feudal corporate abuses.

In an 1864 letter, Abraham Lincoln wrote: *"Corporations have been enthroned and an era of corruption in high places will follow, and the money power of the country will endeavor to prolong its reign by working upon the prejudices of the people until all wealth is aggregated in a few hands and the Republic is destroyed"*

In the U.S. Supreme Court decision of 1886 in Santa Clara County vs. Southern Pacific Railroad, a precedent was set which allowed later court decisions to **designate corporations as** *"natural persons."* This step was crucial in empowering Corporate America, and it is beyond understanding. How can any reasoning and practical person come to the conclusion that a corporate charter creates a human being? Most of the great thinkers of history would be appalled. A piece of paper has human rights? Does it not, then, also have citizen obligations? Can it be drafted into the military or serve on a jury or be imprisoned or executed? Is a corporation ever willing to give up its life for its country? Every moderate in America, nay, every American should be outraged.

It was an easy step from there for the U.S. Supreme Court to strike most local, state and federal laws originally enacted to protect real citizens from corporate excesses. The Fourteenth Amendment was enacted to protect the civil rights of freed slaves, but it was now used to protect the power of the artificial corporate *"persons."* It followed that, as legal *"persons,"* corporations had First Amendment rights as well; hence they could contribute to campaign financing. So it has come that a piece of paper can be a superior, immortal *"person."*

51

Franklin Delano Roosevelt (1882-1945)

The control of the RAP over our system became complete. The Robber Barons were in control. It took the Great Depression, the worst in history, and the New Deal to pass some control back to the citizens.

Adam Smith (Wealth of Nations 1776) opposed corporations. Smith believed that God favored human resourcefulness and industry, and that profits gained in free market were *"natural."* Smith, however, did not regard corporations as a natural part of this system. He argued that large business entities limit competition, and wrote: *"The pretense that corporations are necessary to the better government of the trade is without foundation."*

In 1941, a U.S. Congressional committee stated: ***"The principal instrument of the concentration of economic power and wealth has been the corporate charter with unlimited power."***

These institutions are not flesh and blood and the legal system should acknowledge the fact that corporations are merely one way to do business. They are not *"endowed by the creator with unalienable rights,"* and should not be allowed to influence our elections. In a very realistic way, the imbalance in their enormous size endangers our economy and society. The managerial aristocracies are only gifted people and they will make mistakes or be corrupted by their own greed.

Ominously, the concentration of wealth is now reaching dangerous levels – the levels seen in the 1920's just prior to the Great Depression. From 1976 to 2005 our nation experienced significant growth in wealth; and the share of that wealth owned by the top 1% of our population went from 22% to 39% in that time frame. (See chart page 86.)

The most crippling blow to the economy during the Great Depression was the failure of the banks. Across the country, many banks failed. Because of the general bank failure, laws were passed limiting the potential size of banks and strictly defining their function – safeguard deposits and make prudent loans. Specifying the size of the area they could serve made for size limitations. They were strictly forbidden from crossing political lines. A bank in a city was confined to that city. A bank in a county was confined to that county and could not even enter a city in that county. These practical and prudent laws designed to protect the public from bank failure have been abandoned to lobbyist pressure.

We now have national banks that are also allowed to deal in stocks and act as business consultants. What will happen when a Wachovia, or BankAmerica, or City Bank fails due to managerial mistakes? Many will respond that it can't happen. Well, it almost happened in Japan about a decade ago, forcing that government to step in and save the banks at enormous public cost. A year ago, most would also judge it impossible for General Motors or Ford to possibly approach bankruptcy either.

The free enterprise system works. Two examples of enormous success are Henry Ford and John D. Rockefeller. Both dominated their industries and accumulated enormous wealth, but in different ways. Ford was by providing a good innovative product at a better price than his many competitors. Rockefeller was by swallowing up his competition. The consumer benefited from the enterprise of Ford, but suffered due to the imbalance created by Rockefeller.

It would seem obvious; therefore, that there must be guidelines and regulations so that competition will be to the benefit of the public. Many will argue that the benefit of the public is of secondary importance. Refer again to Adam Smith's *"invisible hand."* His logic that free enterprise is the best system was that is the way to attain the greatest benefit for the public. You cannot advocate a system without advocating its philosophic basis. And, if it is not of primary importance, why is our national goal the *"General Welfare?"*

It is ironic that even the RAP and corporations do not recognize that they are best off when the consuming public is best off. Now, however, not only are the RAP and corporations exerting enormous neofeudal influence on our government, they are actually re-writing the laws; revisions designed to benefit themselves only. They could actually cook our goose laying golden eggs. The banking laws are, perhaps, the most dangerous example; although the new Medicare *"Part D"* may deserve a gold ribbon.

The CosCons have once again been calling for privatization of public services. They want to privatize everything from highways to sewers, from water systems to prisons. They, of course, do not remember the debacle that was the public utility privatization and consolidation of the 1920's. They claim that private enterprise can do it better, but they have little history to back up that claim. And there is specific history that such privatization is dangerous. The deregulation of the natural gas and power industries in the 1990's proved disastrous – ask those who live in California or Montana.

CosCons claim the privatization of industry in Briton under Margaret Thatcher starting in 1979 is sufficient proof of the viability of privatization. The industries that were privatized had been nationalized only few decades before when socialism had gained great popularity in the world during the Great Depression. Reversing a condition to a prior condition proves only the superior viability of the prior condition. It does not prove that the process used for reversal can be universally applied in any or all other areas of human endeavor.

In the early 1920's power utility customers had the availability of many suppliers. Independent generators and distributors competed with public generators and distributors. Streets were a jungle of power lines. This gave way to consolidation and then the rise of huge electric power holding companies which also bought up the public organizations (privatization.) By 1932, almost three-quarters of the nation's investor owned electric business was owned by eight holding companies.

There was no real state or federal regulation. However, it was so chaotic that regulation was necessary and eminent. In 1929, most economic and stock analysts feared that the stock market was overvalued. This included the Federal Reserve (does that not sound familiar – recall Federal Reserve Chairman Greenspan warning of *"irrational exuberance."*) There were many other analysts who felt the market was not overvalued. So, what precipitated the October crash?

Significant as probable triggers were the expansion of public utility holding companies, investment trusts, and heavy margin buying, all of which aided the buying of public utility stocks, and drove prices higher. With the use of large amounts of debt and preferred stock, Public utilities, utility holding companies, and investment trusts were highly leveraged. In October 1929, utility stocks declined sharply. These set off margin calls and panic selling which was then duplicated in the general market.

Black Thursday was October 24, 1929. In a relatively short time, the Dow Jones Industrial Average lost about half its value. The Utility stocks had turned down almost a month earlier. They were the "Dot-Coms" of that time and they led the way down.

History has a way of repeating itself. When the powerful make mistakes, the general public suffers. The threat of Corporate America now is that they are too big and too powerful. The balance is now tilted because corporate wealth dominates the executive and legislative branches of government through campaign contributions. Perhaps they dominate the judicial branch as well. The other elements of checks and balances (principally the state and local government bodies) are also under their domination.

A number of years ago, a prominent, conservative radio talk-show host was asked what had caused the Great Depression. His response was that the cause was government interference with private enterprise. It is interesting, that, according to him, the Great Depression resulted from government interference in a time when there was relatively little government interference. It should be noted it was also a time when the concentration of wealth was at its highest and our government was heavily influenced by the rich and powerful.

More critical, the Federal Reserve was dominated by the private banking industry – they own the Federal Reserve. The damaging loose money policies of the Federal Reserve during the late 1920's and more damaging tight money policies of the early 1930's were implemented by a governing board comprised mostly of New York bankers. They had the support of the Republican government.

It is even more interesting that the current, unprecedented 70 years of prosperity has occurred in a time frame considered to have stifling governmental interference and steeply graduated income tax rates. Perhaps this talk-show host should have been more *"cautious."* Ah, but then he had just demonstrated that he is, without doubt a CosCon since he apparently doesn't know enough history. His politics seem to be based primarily on his *"in the gut"* beliefs.

How does Corporate America fit into the *"Separation of Powers?"*

Sageisms:

"Anyone who is capable of getting themselves made President should on no account be allowed to do the job." -Douglas Adams

"Whereas it has long been known and declared that the poor have no right to the property of the rich, I wish it also to be known and declared that the rich have no right to the property of the poor." -John Ruskin

"What the public wants is called 'politically unrealistic.' Translated into English that means power and privilege are opposed to it."
-Noam Chomsky

Chapter Thirteen
Separation of Powers (SOP)

Baron de la Brède et de Montesquieu (1689-1755)

Montesquieu conceived the *"Separation of Powers"* as a model of democracy involving separating political power into three branches of the state. The executive, the legislative and the judiciary would each have its own specific fields of responsibility. Each branch is also forbidden from exerting power in the field of responsibility of another branch, except that each branch may be empowered to exert checks on the actions of the other branches. Montesquieu coined the phrase *"tres politica,"* and our phrase: *"checks and balances."*

"Checks," according to Montesquieu, were the ability, right and responsibility of each power to monitor the activities of the others. *"Balances"* refers to the ability of each branch to act to limit the powers of the others. It should be obvious that the difference between exerting power in the field of responsibility of another branch and monitoring and limiting the power of another branch is a delicate process. Tradition and public support helps maintain such a system, but also requires balanced tactical positions.

Common law and tradition had created a judicial system and branch steeped in the value of liberty and human rights. This was critical in the development of our system of *"Separation of Powers."*

Maintenance of the *"Separation of Powers"* stems from the separate elections and direct responsibility to the public. Judicial independence is maintained by life appointments, but judges are also susceptible to prejudiced knowledge and corruption. The popular sentiment of the people should constrain the powers of all three branches. National crisis may endanger the *"Separation of Powers,"* so that is when Americans need to be most cautious. Such caution should not be directed abroad; it should be directed toward our own leadership. There have been innumerable examples in history where leaders used foreign threats to usurp and consolidate internal political control. Usually, the system of checks and balances is self-reinforcing. The opportunities for tyranny through a power grab are reduced by the ability of the other two branches to take corrective measures.

In the Federalists papers, James Madison wrote regarding the ability of the branches to defend against the others: *"But it is not possible to give each department an equal power of self-defense. In republican governments the legislative authority necessarily predominates."* This problem was addressed by a bicameral system to reduce the relative power of the legislature. Two houses use different systems of election and rules of action to help protect each against the other. However, when the legislature is unified, it does wield unequal dominate power.

Further enhancing the *"Separation of Powers"* is the very large and inefficient federal bureaucracy. Only the highest level officials are changed with a new President. Also, semi-independent agencies (such as and including the Federal Communications Commission and the Federal Reserve) have been created by the legislature within the executive branch. This *"fourth"* branch of the government enjoys reasonable independence from the other policy makers.

The free press enhances the *"Separation of Powers"* by swaying public opinion which can affect elections. The system of modern day politics may be a further safeguard against any potential abuse of power.

While the form of state and local governments vary widely, they tend to emulate the federal system so they also contribute to the Separation of Powers.

At the lowest level, juries also contribute. They have the sole authority to determine the facts in civil and criminal cases. Thus they act as a buffer against arbitrary enforcement by the judicial or the executive branches. John Lilburne won acquittal by convincing a jury they had the right to find him not guilty because the law he admittedly violated, did not have merit in and of itself. In many areas, Grand Juries have the power to independently investigate government operations.

It all adds up to a system that is effective for liberty, in part, because of its own inefficiency. Everyone who believes in the *"Separation of Powers"* with the essential *"Checks and Balances"* needs to examine the lobbyists system that is threatening America in a most basic way.

In 1941, a U.S. Congressional committee states: *"The principal instrument of the concentration of economic power and wealth has been the corporate charter with unlimited power..."* When the executive and legislative branches are unified and dominated by an outside power the whole system is jeopardized by imbalance and lack of checks. While we ban any person from stuffing our ballot boxes, we have no good way to deter *"stuffing"* money where it corrupts. Montesquieu said: *"There is no greater tyranny than that which is perpetrated under the shield of the law and in the name of justice."*

In most cases, the managements of these corporations are honest men who would not think of cheating on the golf course or in most of their other activities. When it comes to spending money for favors from politicians or bureaucrats, there are no holds barred because that is outside the province of normal ethical behavior. The rational is that it is the only means to achieve certain desired goals. It is the other SOP - *"Standard Operating Procedure."*

For many giant corporations everything comes down to the bottom line – it is Standard Operating Procedure. In the Media Monitors Network issue of 11/21/2006, Peter Rost, an ex-pharmaceutical executive wrote of a corporate practice called *"transfer pricing,"* whereby taxable income is deceptively realized in low tax nations solely to avoid American and Canadian taxes. A straw intermediary buys the foreign produced product at an artificial price and then resells it to the domestic company. The domestic company shows little profit or even a loss, while huge untaxed profits are recorded overseas.

Some of these are the drug companies now advertising on TV about how well they look out for the American public. GlaxoSmithKline recently reached a $3.4 billion settlement with the IRS for a transfer pricing dispute. Merck recently disclosed a potential liability of $5.6 billion to the US and Canada also related to inter-company pricing abuse.

Another tactic used by huge brand-name drug makers is to buy off generic competitors, who agree to stall introduction of cheaper but identical drugs. Two 2005 appeals court decisions upheld the legality of this tactic. The generic manufacturer makes more from this sell-out than from their own sales. Is this *"Laissez-faire"* for the *"General Welfare?"*

Can we trust all corporate reports? To be sure, all profits, foreign or domestic, show up in their accounting reports for evaluation by Wall Street and managerial bonuses; but how much is foreign profits that should be lower domestic profits misstated by this scheme avoiding taxation? How much tax are you paying to make up for the legitimate taxes they are avoiding because it is Standard Operating Procedure? Is this patriotic? Is this moral? Many would regard it as criminal!

Thomas Jefferson said: ***"Merchants have no country. The mere spot they stand on does not constitute so strong an attachment as that from which they draw their gains."*** Machiavelli, deja vu. To be sure,

58

many merchants, corporate or otherwise, are patriotic, moral, frugal and practical; however, many are not and that's the rub.

Corporations are not *"endowed by the creator with unalienable rights,"* and should pay their fair share and should not be allowed to influence our elections, cheat on taxes or buy off competition. The American consumer pays all the bills, whether it is our taxes or the dollars we spend every day that eventually passes through the hands of the corporations. People, real people, should make the big decisions.

A system of *"equality of sacrifice"* taxes yields two distinct practical benefits. First it has proven to defeat the concentration of wealth. Second, and more important, it puts additional money in the hands of the spenders insuring continued prosperity. It creates balance.

The battle between the Federalists (elitists) and Republican-Democrats (populists) was fought and won over 200 years ago. It needs to be fought again. Ironically, the very class of men that now personify the danger – our managerial aristocracy - will agree. They simply don't see the danger for three reasons:

First, corporations are judged solely by bottom line success.

Second, they believe that their acts which endanger our system are justified by no more than this goal of success. It is *"Standard Operating Procedure"* to seduce politicians with campaign contributions, to avoid any and all taxation legally and otherwise, and to minimize worker's pay and benefits, while maximizing their own.

Third, most importantly, they have a limited knowledge of history.

The *"Separation of Powers"* is one of our most basic standards, yet it is now compromised by the imbalance inherent in the enormous wealth and influence of Corporate America. There is danger from both sides of the aisle because of dependence by politicians on corporate campaign contributions. Quid pro quo garners legislation specifically benefiting Corporate America to the detriment of the public interest. Corruption has again reared its ugly head and it will continue to do so until we, as a nation, restore the *"Separation of Powers."*

There are dangerous immortals among us run by usually good and honest men, but one should never assume that they want a smaller, more efficient government. Montesquieu said: *"Government should be set up so that no man need be afraid of another"* The people of America have good reason to be afraid of the *"persons"* that are our corporations. The *"Separation of Powers"* can, and may now be compromised by *"Standard Operating Procedure."* They should be numbered (SOP[1] and SOP[2]) so we will never forget which is paramount. Who's driving?

Who'$ Driving?

Chapter Fourteen
"The Human Story"

In 2004, history Professor James C. Davis published his worthwhile book: *"The Human Story."* (ISBN 0-06-051619-4) It covers mankind's history from the Stone Age to recent times. It often details the horrors perpetrated on common man by powerful men seeking great wealth or increased power. While only 440 pages of easy reading, it is summarized by an astonishing sixteen line epilog verse.

In the epilog, Professor Davis speaks of man's life worldwide being harsh and without freedom; primitive homes invariably had insect and rodent infestations and child mortality was high – bewailed by holy men as the *"will of God."* With the advent of personal liberty, inventions, innovations and medical progress, our lot, like rising tides, improved and our lives lengthened. We shed ourselves of tyrannical governments peacefully or otherwise; and then we reached for the stars. Scientific progress compounded, and while there are still many problems and dangers, the past was definitely worse. He uses the common expression *"so far so good"* as his epilog's title and concluding thought.

Just consider all of the wars that man has fought over the ages and all around the world – most were and still are motivated by the ambition of strong men to gain wealth or power. Try to assign a value to wars from the perspective of history - which wars were meaningful and have left a lasting positive impact on mankind?

Maybe you can regard four as qualified for that standard: the French and American Revolutions, the Civil War and World War II. Certainly, there were others but not with lasting significance. **These are the only wars that were primarily about human liberty.**

Then consider all the positive developments in mankind's history – inventions, innovations and medical progress. From personal liberty, to moral amelioration, to medical advances, to scientific discoveries, to innovations and inventions; how many of those developments can be attributed to the rich and powerful? Certainly, many of those responsible for innovations and inventions joined the ranks of the rich and powerful, but only after the fact. Many important early inventions and innovations, like inalienable rights, were lost in antiquity to declining liberty.

The rich and powerful have now convinced the CosCons to want a return to old ways, forgetting that old times were much worse. *"Once was worse"* is the battle cry of those who view politics in a historical perspective. *"So far so good"* is not just a victory celebration, it is a declaration of war for posterity.

Joining the rich and powerful in their onslaught on our system is the religious right: (holy men and the Will of God.) The religious accident of life has historically often made things worse. Look at the lack of liberty in the theocratic nations around the world. How should the 97% Muslims in Iraq treat the 3% Christian minority? How should we treat our 14% who are non-Christians? Our Founding Fathers, with good reason, provided us the answer.

Arnold Toynbee said: *"It is a great law of social development that the movement from slavery to freedom is also a movement from security to insecurity of maintenance."* Our lot has improved and our lives have lengthened like rising tides. Be ever mindful that tides fall as well as rise. History's rising tide is liberty; the falling tide is the restriction of liberty *("insecurity of maintenance.")* because it is *"necessary."*

All who want to preserve liberty should be aware that *"necessity"* is a plea by the powerful for increased control over common men. William Pitt, a British statesman in 1783 warned: *"It is the argument of tyrants. It is the creed of slaves."* Ironically, he later tried to have Thomas Paine arrested for sedition.

Spreading liberation of humans is having other benefits. The number of armed conflicts in the world has declined significantly since the end of the cold war. While terrorism may be on the rise, 2004 had the lowest number of civil conflicts in almost 30 years. The number of deaths attributable to wars is also declining dramatically.

Freedom House recently published its 2005 Global *"Freedom in the World"* survey. Looking at civil liberties around the world, the survey finds improvement in freedom of the press, the rights of women and the rule of law. For the rest of the world to get there, we must make very sure America stays there. So far so good!

Another recommended book is Jim Powell's *"The Triumph of Liberty."* (ISBN 0-684-85967-X) The book's bias to *"Libertarian"* political ideals in no way detracts from its value as a source of historical information. Refreshing society's memory of forgotten heroes like John Lilburne and Mary Wollstonecraft underlines this book's contention that history is repetitious because it is forgotten.

The libertarian love affair with *"Laissez-faire"* capitalism ignores history's lesson concerning the dangers found in the concentration of wealth in very few hands. The political power that accompanies concentration of wealth presents the greatest danger to the libertarian's highest ideal of personal liberty yet it is the natural result of the *"Laissez-faire"* capitalism which is central to their highest ideal of personal liberty. This dangerous circuity must not be ignored.

Mahatma Gandhi said: *"The things that will destroy us are: politics without principle; pleasure without conscience; wealth without work; knowledge without character; business without morality; science without humanity; and worship without sacrifice."* Cogitate upon this quote and identify those aspects of our society that have the potential to destroy our system. In particular think about *"politics without principle"* and *"business without morality"* – they are connected through SOP[2] campaign financing provided by lobbyists for the Nonservatives.

It should be noted that the George W. Bush administration, in addition to fudging on Constitutional guarantees of privacy, has also violated traditional patriotic frugality. In all major conflicts, with the exception of the 1846 Mexican-American War, the American people were asked to make patriotic financial sacrifices. Not only are our finest on the ground fighting this war, they will be asked to pay for it during the balance of their working years. The Iraq war *"is being fought on our children's shoulders,"* said Judd Gregg, a top Republican. *"You're probably talking about around $750 billion that is going to be spent on this war that will end up not being funded."*

Are the RAP responsible for the progress mankind has made or are they merely the prime beneficiaries? To be sure, they have managed the lives of many and they dominate the history books and some did, admittedly, manage well. All reasoning people, however, should reach the conclusion that while the rich and powerful run things, they have historically most often ruined things. The difference between run and ruin is just, and it is, indeed, a very small letter.

Sageisms:

"Official Announcement: The government today announced that it is changing its emblem from an Eagle to a CONDOM because it more accurately reflects the government's political stance. A condom allows for inflation, halts production, destroys the next generation, protects a bunch of pricks, and gives you a sense of security while you're actually being screwed. It just doesn't get more accurate than that!" -Anonymous

"Political necessities sometime turn out to be political mistakes."
-George Bernard Shaw

Chapter Fifteen
Democracies End

Aristotle's "polity" was rule by the many, who are neither wealthy nor poor, in the interests of the whole community - the ideal form of government somewhere between oligarchy and democracy.

Aristotle (384-322 BC)

We all want our grandchildren and their grandchildren to have liberty. There are, however, many examples where liberty has ended. In ancient times, the best examples are the Athenian democracy and Rome.

The former is referred to as the *"classical democracy."* It included the city of Athens and surrounding Attica. All the citizens voted on legislation; and while not all of the inhabitants had the franchise, there were no exclusions by economic class and virtually all citizens participated as their franchise included a duty to participate. Most historians date this democracy from 508 BC to 322 BC when it fell to Macedonian conquerors – external political power.

Alexander the Great defeated some democracies in India. It is possible that the current success of democracy in India has foundation in that tradition of historic democracies. Arrian's *"Anabasis of Alexander"* gives accounts of Alexander conquering several *"free and independent"* Indian communities.

The Roman system was an interesting political mixture of elected Consuls serving for one year and life serving Senators. Two Consuls, elected by the army, were the military and civil authorities; after which they joined the Senate for life and served in an advisory capacity. Legislation was enacted by all the citizens.

The Roman Revolution filled almost a century before the end of the Republic. Military leaders, administrating conquered lands for many years, wanted independence from Rome because much of the wealth was exported back to Rome concentrating in the hands of the Senators. This great concentration of wealth corrupted their democratic system and many citizens sold their franchise or were driven from their property. Following the assassination of Caesar, Octavian ended the republic when he marched on Rome and annulled the powers of the Senate.

The city of Rome was the largest population center of that time, numbering around one million people. Historical estimates indicate that possibly a third of the population under the jurisdiction of ancient Rome lived in cities with populations of 10,000 and more, certainly a high rate of urbanization for that time. These people were much like us, except for the 20 to 40% who were slaves.

In modern times, the best example of failed democracy is Germany, but many South American democracies turned to dictatorships or "strong man" dominated democracies after the Cuban revolution. It was their way of guarding the wealthy from socialism and communism. Several European democracies similarly fell following the Russian revolution.

The imbalance found in the hard times of the global economic Great Depression following World War I led to strange marriages of rabble rousing hate mongers and the elite of industry. The wealthy protected their assets and the popular revisionists got backing. For the people of those nations, these were marriages made in hell.

Fascism's answer to the Great Depression was to embrace society's wealthiest individuals by favoring certain corporations, ending constitutional rights and stifling dissent. They also resorted to war to stimulate economic growth. America, on the other hand, used minimum wage legislation to support the middle class, curtailed the unbalanced power of corporations with anti-trust enforcement, implemented a steeply graduated income tax, created Social Security and began many public works programs.

Fascism is defined as: *"a political philosophy, movement or regime that exalts nation and often race above the individual and that stands for a centralized autocratic government headed by a dictatorial leader, severe economic and social regimentation, and forcible suppression of opposition."*

The question is not whether democracy can come to an end in America; the question is whether economic conditions can become so severely depressed in America so as to bring democracy to an end. In Germany, all it took was severe economic depression combined with a terrorist attack. We cannot foresee another Great Depression but virtually no one could in the past either. We now have all the ingredients that Hitler had except the depression.

Who'$ Driving?

What might happen if a few of our largest corporations should bankrupt, or if some of our largest banks should fail, or if Social Security goes busted, or if foreign investor nations cease financing our National Debt, or any number of natural disasters, or the collapse of the stock market? We have no way of knowing if prosperity will continue, but the odds are high something will happen sooner or later.

It is now forgotten that at the depth of the depression there was serious debate and wide support for implementing many socialist programs – as actually happened in Great Britain. The New Deal was critical in curtailing that movement and in maintaining democracy and capitalism in America, as was the fact that we were still largely an agrarian society.

Those living on farms did not feel the devastating effects of depression like city dwellers: *a neighbor of the author, relates how as a young girl in rural Georgia, her father would read the comic section of the newspaper to her and her sister on a porch swing every Sunday morning. One day, during the depression, he showed the girls a picture on the front page of a "bread line" in Atlanta. After pointing out that because of the advantage of living on a farm they would never have to worry about hunger, he read them the comics.*

Adolph Hitler (1889-1945)

When the next depression comes, are we going to have another FDR or are we going to have another Adolph Hitler? We do have an upper class of extreme wealth and a managerial aristocracy that will be highly interested in safeguarding their property in the face of a spreading socialist movement that goes with every depression.

We also have another key ingredient that Hitler had in his bid for control – an unpopular minority tainted by the label of terrorists. It was a terrorist fire bombing of the German Parliament (Reichstag) building on February 27, 1933 that legitimized Hitler and ended the German republic as a democracy.

The Dutch terrorist, Marinus van der Lubbe (a mentally unstable communist,) was known to the German intelligence. As was common in multi-party European democracies, Hitler had not been elected by a majority vote. After the bombing, Hitler declared: *"You are now witnessing the beginning of a great epoch in history, this fire is the beginning."* He called it a *"sign from God,"* and declared an all-out war on the terrorist sponsors. Hitler had his Jews and we have our Muslims.

Shortly thereafter construction began on a detention camp for terrorists in Oranianberg and legislation was enacted ending basic constitutional guarantees. Police could wiretap phones, suspected terrorists could be imprisoned without charges or access to legal defense.

Key Nazi government posts were filled by former executives of the largest corporations. Government money was diverted to subsidize corporations so they could help him fight the war against the Middle Eastern ancestry terrorists. Hitler then embraced two wars as a diversion from internal and foreign opposition.

After a brief and successful invasion first of Austria and then of Czechoslovakia involving little loss of German blood, Hitler became a popular national hero, was hailed around the world and even honored by Time Magazine as the *"Man of the Year."*

A nationwide campaign was begun charging his critics with attacking Germany itself. Those opposing him were labeled *"not good Germans"* (our *"anti-American"*) and accused them of aiding the enemy by not supporting the valiant troops in uniform. The *"intellectuals and liberals"* who opposed him became enemies of the state.

These events have an eerie familiarity. **Say *"liberty's loss can't happen here"* and then put your self in the shoes of a Roman citizen about 30 BC and repeat it in Latin or the shoes of a German in 1933 and say *"Sieg Heil."*** Democracies mostly have come to and end when the rich and powerful feel threatened. History is repetitive and it would seem prudent to stand a close watch for any and all developments that could jeopardize liberty. Violation of human rights is often the rule when powerful people protect what is theirs, even if their possession is no more than a theory or a belief. Beliefs come in many colors.

Crayons

Each day shaded by problems
Dark or light, each is a test
Preoccupation and worry condemns
Us to turmoil; minds rarely at rest
All are easy or hard to solve
It depends on how we view them

Who'$ Driving?

It depends on our own resolve
Our attitude as we work through them
Color our books; try to stay in the lines
Find in each challenge some fun
Each problem our attitude defines
As an opportunity to get something done
Our heritage draws the outline
Our values determine the way
Each crayon used, the choice condign
As we watchfully color each day

Sageisms:

"He who would make his own liberty secure must guard even his enemy from oppression; for if he violates this duty he establishes a precedent that will reach to himself." -Thomas Paine

"A government big enough to give you everything you want, is strong enough to take everything you have." -Thomas Jefferson

"There is no distinctly native American criminal class...save Congress." -Mark Twain

"Practical politics consists in ignoring facts." -Henry Brooks Adams

"The only justifiable purpose of political institutions is to ensure the unhindered development of the individual." -Albert Einstein

"The stronger side will dictate its own terms; and as a matter of fact, in the early days of competition the capitalists used all their power to oppress the labourers, and drove down wages to starvation point." -Arnold Toynbee

"I must study politics and war that my sons may have liberty to study mathematics and philosophy." -John Adams

"So potent was religion in persuading to evil deeds." –Lucretius

"Our lives begin to end the day we become silent about things that matter." - Martin Luther King Jr.

Chapter Sixteen
Theories in Conflict

There can be little doubt that the most discredited economist of all time is Karl Marx, as he should be.

Karl Marx (1818-1883)

Marxism holds the belief that free enterprise allows the exploitation of workers by the owners of capital, and private ownership of the means of production restricts worker's freedom. Employers must pay employees less than the value their labor creates and Marx called that exploitation. Marx argued that capitalism has built-in contradictions that must lead to its collapse. He saw capitalism as a stage in the evolution of human society.

Adam Smith (1723-1790)

The *"Father of Capitalism,"* Adam Smith argued that private businessmen would give the people what they want in order to make money by following their own self-interest. Such self interest is commonly regarded as playing an essential role in capitalism. People pursuing their own self interest are compensated by the public for their labor in a voluntary exchange. Smith termed this mutual activity the *"invisible hand"* and said it would guide people to act in the public interest: Smith wrote: *"By pursuing his own interest, an individual frequently promotes that of the society more effectually than when he really intends to promote it."*

Who'$ Driving?

Capitalism is the belief that private ownership is essential to enriching society as well as preserving personal freedom. Capitalism is that economic system whereby the means of production are mostly owned and operated by private interests. Further, the investment of capital, the production, distribution and prices of commodities, and the provision of services are determined primarily by a free market. The driving force is the profit motive. Essential to the capitalist theory is the concept of *"Laissez-faire"*

"Laissez-faire" means *"let do, let go, let pass"* in French and is what we generally refer to as *"free market."* True conservatives should embrace the concept as a doctrine opposing governmental interference with trade, and opposing economic intervention and taxation beyond that which is perceived necessary to insure peace, prosperity, security, property rights and liberty. Their theory is that a free market, unconstrained by government, will achieve efficiencies unattainable under any other system so government should stay out of economic decisions like production, distribution, pricing and consumption of goods and services by the private sector. Conservatives should also embrace the concept as a doctrine opposing interference with government by powerful private interests. *"Laissez-faire"* must be a two-way street.

While Smith went far in making *"Laissez-faire"* economics broadly accepted, the philosophy he set forth became corrupted. *"Laissez-faire,"* according to Smith, does not mean *"pro-business."* Government that is pro-active in support of business should be as undesirable to a true conservative as government that is pro-active the adult poor and working classes. Corporate welfare is even more obnoxious than the *"war on poverty"* welfare handouts to the poorest in our nation. This is the case because business can and have used corporate welfare benefits to corrupt public officials in order to obtain even greater benefits.

CosCons, unfortunately, see no difference between pro-active business and *"Laissez-faire."* **The conservative value endorsing** *"small government"* **demands that government not embrace pro-active business or labor policies.** The beneficiaries of pro-active government can and have gained economic and political power that, in the past, has always endangered conservative values.

"Laissez-faire" economics has flaws especially when certain key industrial areas are dominated by cartels in restraint of trade as witnessed in the world from oil embargos in the 1970s and 2005. Huge corporate conglomerates are, by their very nature, monopolistic cartels having reached their great size often through purchase of competitors rather than

by competition. This very same kind of imbalance in the 1920's was the key factor leading to the Great Depression.

Arguments that *"Laissez-faire"* policies cause the Great Depression are as fruitless as arguments that it was economic regulation by the government. The truth is that it was probably *"Laissez-faire"* and pro-active business policies by the Federal Reserve that led to that depression combined with an excessive concentration of wealth.

LamLibs do not take history sufficiently into account yet bewail the favoritism shown by government to the business community as they should since the favoritism goes to those businesses with the greatest political clout. But, LamLibs also demand favoritism wanting the government to solve all sorts of social ills by spending money. Such programs rarely accomplish the desired goals and, more often, may defeat what is intended – welfare being the best case in point. Many of the LamLib goals further enrich the powerful as it is often they who implement many liberal programs – for instance, nursing homes.

Government pro-active business policies include direct subsidies to businesses, agricultural products, and regulation of market competition, trade barriers by tariffs or quotas, and other forms of favoritism. These do not fit in classic *"Laissez-faire"* theory. Perhaps, the term itself has become more a political tool than anything else, covering the pro-active business activities of the government and obscuring the economic imperialism of corporate America. Many believe that *"Laissez-faire"* endorses government favoritism of business, but nothing could be further from the truth. *"Laissez-faire"* must be a two-way street.

The lessons of history are that government intervention is necessary to prevent the growth of monopolies and oversight is needed to combat fraud and worse. *"Laissez-faire"* does not mean no *"oversight."* We are, after all, a nation where the rule of law and order is highly valued by all. There is no basis to argue against the concept of *"Laissez-faire"* other than the need to recognize that communal activities outside of business and religion demand *"Laissez-faire"* standards. Democratic government is business exclusively *"for the people"* and other interests should be constrained from interfering in the business of the people.

Why are the interests of society more important? Simply because that is what we all want. It is not your selfish motive for yourself; it is what you want for your grandchildren and for their grandchildren. You may make a great fortune through you selfish activities, but when your grandchildren fritter it away, you want their children and grandchildren to have the opportunity to succeed just as you succeeded. To ensure that opportunity, we must make sure that the conservative standards we hold highest will be there for them.

There can be no doubt that America has witnessed the development of the largest middle class in the world since the implementation of Roosevelt's *"New Deal,"* the enormous expansion of the military-industrial complex, and public works like the interstate highway system and NASA. This process enriched our entire society, but political power has shifted and the concentration of wealth is accelerating.

Our problem is to make sure that our system is stable and safe. That is the public interest. Public interest is not welfare and not pork, but it is a safe environment, it is clean air and safe streets and decent pay and working conditions and safe food and good schools and so many other things. It is, most certainly, not found in the concentration of wealth.

Every historic democracy came to an end including more than a score in the 1900s alone. Historically the greatest threat to democracy has been political power based on concentration of wealth in few hands and Corporate America now poses that threat to our liberties. Plutarch said: *"An imbalance between rich and poor is the oldest and most fatal ailment of all republics."* Ours can be different only if we make sure that all potential dangers are contained and balance maintained.

There you have it: the economic theory extremes that can and have torn the world apart. *"Laissez-faire capitalism"* – focused on the role of enlightened self-interest (the *"invisible hand"*) versus public ownership of the means of production.

That does not mean, however, that Smith was completely correct nor that Marx was completely wrong. That argument will rage on and on. Marx's analysis that uncontrolled capitalism will lead to a concentration of wealth in fewer and fewer hands is reasonable and reflected in actual history. His further insightful conclusion that such concentration must eventually stifle the competition necessary for healthy capitalism also seems reasonable and is reflected in actual history. History has proven, without doubt, that capitalism is the superior system, but supervision and control by government is necessary to insure its proper operation. On *"Laissez-faire"* capitalism, Arnold Toynbee said: *"a stream whose strength and direction have to be observed, that embankments may be thrown up within which it may do its work harmlessly and beneficially."*

Keep in mind the irony seen in the growth and dominance of Corporate America is that it occurred under a political system roundly condemned by CosCons as too controlling. As it turned out, Corporate

Who'$ Driving?

America was probably the primary long term beneficiary of the New Deal, which was inspired by the Great Depression of the early 1930's which in turn was devastating over the short term for the average American. Many needlessly lost their life savings and their position in the middle class.

A side product of the New Deal was the curtailment of a broad socialist movement sweeping our nation. The New Deal instituted controls on corporate America and the concentration of wealth. Only then did the world and especially America accumulate wealth to the extreme. **All should recognize that spreading the wealth is beneficial to everyone including the rich and powerful.**

History has demonstrated the reasonableness of some of Marx's analysis – not his conclusions. You need consider our system of industrial America where huge, immortal corporations choose not to compete in the classic sense. You need also consider seriously the managerial aristocratic class that exercises enormous influence over our government. The managerial aristocracy as a class, like every other class, is not fit to govern. Are political preferences meaningful? Who is driving?

Sageisms:

"The first panacea for a mismanaged nation is inflation of the currency; the second is war. Both bring a temporary prosperity; both bring a permanent ruin. But both are the refuge of political and economic opportunists." -Ernest Hemingway

"When the tyrant has disposed of foreign enemies by conquest or treaty, and there is nothing to fear from them, then he is always stirring up some war or other in order that the people may require a leader." –Plato

"History is past politics, and politics is present history." -E. A. Freeman

"Any excuse will serve a tyrant." -Aesop

"Political necessities sometime turn out to be political mistakes." -George Bernard Shaw

"Patriotism is not 'loving your government'. A patriot is one who loves his country and watches his government." – F. Tupper Saussy

Chapter Seventeen
Political Preferences

The inequities found in any democratic and capitalist system are essential to making the system fluid and stable. The inequities found in the more mature of such systems, like the aged's hardening of the arteries, can debilitate the fluidity and destabilize both the capitalism and the democracy. One such inequity that appears to be especially beneficial to the health of the system is the *"equality of sacrifice"* in relative tax burden. The greatest prosperity and stability in history has occurred under the most severely graduated income tax rates which apparently facilitated a flow of wealth down the social structure and made possible more upward mobility among the classes.

Maturing also impairs eyesight and depth perception – necessitating only right turns on the highways of life. Michael Gartner, who won the Pulitzer Prize for Editorial Writing, tells an amusing and insightful story of his parents in a column in USA Today. In summery, his father, Carl Gartner, quit driving a car in 1927 at age 25. He did buy a car for his oldest son in 1951, and his wife started driving at the age of 43 in 1952. For 75 years, Carl did not drive and went to work on foot or by trolley. The whole family apparently did a lot of walking.

Until his mother was 90, she did all the driving while Carl served as navigator which worked well. He went with her on all outings. When Carl was 95, he told Michael his secret for a long life: **no left turns.** Carl and his wife had read an article that claimed most accidents involving the elderly occurred while making left turns in front of oncoming traffic. The article said the elderly lose depth perception, so Carl and his wife decided to never make left turns. They would make three right turns instead – a practical, if not frugal, solution.

In the column, Michael Gartner related that his father had paid $3,000 for the home they moved into in 1937. Some time in the late 1990's, the two sons had a shower installed in the home at a cost of almost three times the original price of the home. He said his father would probably have died then if he had known the cost of the shower. Carl survived to the age of 102 and died peacefully. Michael Gartner could not attribute Carl's long life to the fact that he walked so much or to the fact that he quit making any left turns. America should consider making only right turns.

There is an old story of a condemned criminal granted a stay of execution because he claimed he could teach the king's horse to sing a hymn within one year. And so, he sat daily singing a hymn to the king's horse. The other convicts laughed at him, until one day he was asked why he did it. His answer was that no one knows what can happen in a year? He could die, the king could die, the horse could die, or even the horse could learn to sing a hymn.

And who knows what could happen in the next year. Perhaps, even the CosCons among us may learn they have been duped by their leadership into concentrating wealth and power in the hands of the few; a condition which has historically ended democracies. The CosCons buy the inalienable political fabrications of their leadership because they want to believe. They selectively remember *"Laissez-Faire," "Natural Rights," "Separation of Powers"* and *"Checks and Balances,"* but they have forgotten so many other important ideas from history. What exactly do CosCons want to conserve that can possibly justify putting our liberty and our democracy in harm's way?

Perhaps, even the LamLibs among us may learn that they have been deceived by their leadership into wanting powerful government and unrealistic limitations on private enterprise. Aristotle said: ***"The worst form of inequality is to try to make unequal things equal"*** What levels of fairness do LamLibs want that can justify putting our liberty and our democracy in harm's way? They selectively remember *"Do unto others," "Natural Rights," "Separation of Powers"* and *"Checks and Balances,"* but they fail to recognize that inequities are essential to the capitalist system and they have forgotten so many other important ideas from history. What exactly do LamLibs want to change that might not undermine the capitalism and private property that are essential aspects of liberty and our democratic system?

To be sure, some governmental limitations on private enterprise are necessary. Moderates recognize that the rule of law is an essential part of our natural rights in the pursuit of happiness. Lines must be drawn and the debate is about where these lines should be placed. Strictly speaking, extortion is, in essence, a form of free enterprise, yet the line is drawn. The feudal system was basically extortion. Monopolistic cartels are feudal in nature and, therefore, anti-American.

Too many citizens base their political preferences on observation, logic and learned precedents without tempering that with the lessons of history. We must maintain our economic and political system and insure liberty, prosperity and tranquility while facilitating frugality.

LamLibs ignore the lessons of history, see inequities, governmental abuses and high taxes, but cannot see that the government spending money rarely solves problems. The CosCons see too much government and high taxes (in feudal societies, taxes could run as high as 80 %.) Moreover, the Christian right, forgetting *"do unto others"* and the terrors and misery of religious discrimination and domination, is trying to unify all Christian voters to impose their *"hallowed"* beliefs on our system.

LamLibs, traditionalists and CosCons alike ignore, at our peril, the lessons of history. **A key, inalienable observation from history is the greatest progress politically, economically and morally has been made possibly only because of the increase and spread of personal liberty.**

Since liberty is our most prized possession, it must be maintained at the highest possible level and that requires constant vigilance. Political power is the only serious threat to liberty and any threat, internal or external, is unacceptable. Plutocracy is government by the wealthy, or by a government primarily influenced by the wealthy, and is against any principle of individual liberty. Our current American political system can be criticized because of the excessive influence of the rich. This should not be mistaken as a criticism of capitalism or of wealth. It is a criticism of the imbalance in concentrated political power.

Many celebrated thinkers and statesmen of the past have warned of the dangers in concentration of wealth in few hands. Historically, liberty has been curtailed when the rich and powerful controlling a democratic government feel their possessions are threatened. Will and Ariel Durant astutely made an important observation: *"Concentration of wealth is a natural result of concentration of ability, and recurs in history. The rate of concentration varies (other factors being equal) with the economic freedom permitted by morals and the law ... democracy, allowing the most liberty, accelerates it."*

Plutarch warned against imbalance. The concentration of wealth is a non-sustainable progression since the gains are always at the expense of all the lower classes. A point will be reached where balance is lost. We are now reaching the point of wealth concentration where severe depressions have occurred in the past. Greatly disadvantaged people will embrace violence. The rich and powerful will react with purchased, superior violence curtailing the civil rights of those below them. Poverty is the womb of discontent; discontent is the mother of democratic or violent social(ist) reform; social reformation is an unacceptable threat to great wealth; any serious threat to great wealth is potentially the death knell of liberty. More important: a concentration of wealth can stifle economic growth by reducing the ability to consume by the multitude.

Who'$ Driving?

Look at the world today. Where do you see the most liberty? Where do you see the strongest economies that are not based on natural resources? Where do you see the greatest wealth based on natural resources? **Those nations whose economies are based primarily on oil and other natural resources have the greatest concentration of wealth and the least liberty.**

Saudi Arabia has 261.9 billion barrels of oil reserves. It is a monarchy with highly restricted civil rights and no religious freedom. Canada has 178.8 billion barrels and is the exception because their liberty came before the demand for oil. Iran has 125.7 billion barrels and is a theocracy with little rights for their minority religions. Iraq has 115 billion barrels and does not now have a repressive dictatorship only because of the intervention by the United States. Kuwait is perhaps one of the better situations with a benevolent monarchy. The United Arab Emirates also has some favorable aspects. Venezuela is rapidly degenerating into strong man control. What is happening now in Russia is confirmation that liberty is precious and threatened by the concentration of wealth. Russia embraced capitalism, more or less, but had no checks for the concentration of wealth which proceeded at an accelerated rate to the point that the super-wealthy tried to challenge Putin's power. At least one of the super-wealthy was jailed.

What do all these nations, except Canada, have in common? They are dominated either by the very wealthy, a politically powerful strong man, or by powerful religious leadership. If you look at the countries of the world listed by their per capita Gross Domestic Product, the top oil rich nation is Canada in 15th position. The United Arab Emirates is 34th and you have to go all the way down to 69th to find Saudi Arabia. Of the 226 nations listed, the top half contains mostly democracies and the bottom half has few democracies. The top half has religious freedom while the others do not as a rule. The top half respects the rights of women and minorities and the others do not.

We no longer have the Cold War between a dictatorship and the Western Democracies, but we do have an economic war. We have *"inalienable rights"* and they have totalitarian control. We have, more or less, respect for the rights of minorities and they have intolerance. We have what is mostly right in the world and they have the oil. We have to kowtow to them because we need the oil. **The curse of having enormous natural resources is that the rich and powerful will horde the benefits of the resources for themselves.** They can only maintain that by restricting the rights of those below them in the social scale. **This is practical proof of the danger found in the concentration of wealth.**

Looking at Gross Domestic Product per capita confirms the relationship between free nations and prosperity. The top twenty are all western democracies with the exception of Australia, Japan and Qatar, (the only one that is not a democracy.) Unfortunately, GDP does not measure the sustainability of growth. For instance, the people of Nauru, a republic island east of New Zealand in the Pacific Ocean, had one of the highest per capita income levels until 1989 when their phosphate mines ran out. What happens when oil runs out?

Ronald Reagan's
Farwell Address to the Nation
January 11, 1989

"Finally, there is a great tradition of warnings in presidential farewells, and I've got one that's been on my mind for some time.

"Ours was the first revolution in the history of mankind that truly reversed the course of government, and with three little words: "We the people." "We the people" tell the government what to do, it doesn't tell us. "We the people" are the driver, the government is the car. And we decide where it should go, and by what route, and how fast. Almost all the world's constitutions are documents in which governments tell the people what their privileges are. Our Constitution is a document in which "We the people" tell the government what it is allowed to do "We the people" are free.

"An informed patriotism is what we want. And are we doing a good enough job teaching our children what America is and what she represents in the long history of the world? Those of us who are over 35 or so years of age grew up in a different America. We were taught, very directly, what it means to be an American. And we absorbed, almost in the air, a love of country and an appreciation of its institutions. If you didn't get these things from your family, you got them from the neighborhood, from the father down the street who fought in Korea or the family who lost someone at Anzio. Or you could get a sense of

patriotism from school. And if all else failed, you could get a sense of patriotism from popular culture. The movies celebrated democratic values and implicitly reinforced the idea that America was special. TV was like that, too, through the mid-'60s.

"But now, we're about to enter the '90s, and some things have changed. Younger parents aren't sure that an unambivalent appreciation of America is the right thing to teach modern children. And as for those who create the popular culture, well-grounded patriotism is no longer the style. Our spirit is back, but we haven't reinstitutionalized it. We've got to do a better job of getting across that America is freedom--freedom of speech, freedom of religion, freedom of enterprise. And freedom is special and rare. It's fragile; it needs protection. . ... "So, we've got to teach history based not on what's in fashion but what's important: Why the Pilgrims came here, who Jimmy Doolittle was, and what those 30 seconds over Tokyo meant." – The Great Communicator.

What makes sustainable growth and wealth is surely a frugal, productive, consuming population! To a minor extent this results from investment, but, over time, almost all investment comes from earnings derived from the consumption of the many items created by innovation and invention. The best and only way to maximize the wealth of any nation is by maximizing consumption by the entire populous.

It is ironic that most of the main contentions to be found in this book, which CosCons may erroneously judge to be liberal, are echoes of Ronald Reagan's farewell speech. The difference is that their Nonservatism does not recognize the importance of history and gives little weight, if any, to the necessity of social morality, practicality and frugality. It is curious that the CosCons who idolize Reagan choose not to remember the more important thoughts dominating his farewell speech. Political preferences should be based largely on history,

The book's contention that morality and history are forgotten although they are essential in reaching political judgments echoes Reagan's: *"I'm warning of an eradication of the American memory that could result, ultimately, in an erosion of the American spirit. Let's start with some basics: more attention to American history and a greater emphasis on civic ritual."*

The book's contention that liberty is of prime value and always at risk echoes Reagan's *"We've got to do a better job of getting across that America is freedom--freedom of speech, freedom of religion, freedom of enterprise. And freedom is special and rare. It's fragile; it needs protection."*

Who'$ Driving?

The book's contention that moral, frugal and practical policies are important echoes Reagan's *"I've been asked if I have any regrets. Well, I do. The deficit is one."* And: *"First, I'm out there stumping to help future presidents - Republican or Democrat - get those tools they need to bring the budget under control. And those tools are a line-item veto and a constitutional amendment to balance the budget."*

Among the many memories we need in the battle to conserve our inalienable rights is Lincoln's Gettysburg Address, November 19, 1863:

Abraham Lincoln (1809-1865)

"Four score and seven years ago our fathers brought forth on this continent, a new nation, conceived in Liberty, and dedicated to the proposition that all men are created equal." *Now we are engaged in a great civil war, testing whether that nation, or any nation so conceived and so dedicated, can long endure. We are met on a great battle-field of that war. We have come to dedicate a portion of that field, as a final resting place for those who here gave their lives that that nation might live. It is altogether fitting and proper that we should do this.*

*But, in a larger sense, we can not dedicate -- we can not consecrate -- we can not hallow -- this ground. The brave men, living and dead, who struggled here, have consecrated it, far above our poor power to add or detract. The world will little note, nor long remember what we say here, but it can never forget what they did here. It is for us the living, rather, to be dedicated here to the unfinished work which they who fought here have thus far so nobly advanced. It is rather for us to be here dedicated to the great task remaining before us -- that from these honored dead we take increased devotion to that cause for which they gave the last full measure of devotion -- that we here highly resolve that these dead shall not have died in vain -- that this nation, under God, shall have a new birth of freedom -- **and that government of the people, by the people, for the people, shall not perish from the earth."***

Both Reagan's and Lincoln's words underline the preeminence of liberty and government *"of the people, by the people, for the people."* If we want our system to have a long life, we need to quit making left turns.

Who'$ Driving?

Our conservative values of morality, frugality and practicality must come to fore. This highway of life is too heavily trafficked for us to take risks with the future. The neofeudal favoritism for special interests is a convoy of heavily laden enormous trucks, exceeding reasonably size and weight limits. Our driver's many left turns finds us on the wrong side of the road and that convoy of trucks is coming right at us. The practical safety of making only right turns is ignored.

Lao Tzu (6th century BC)

Lao Tzu, a philosopher observed, *"Those who have knowledge don't predict. Those who predict don't have knowledge."* Predicting that future history will repeat past history will bear no fear of contradiction or of being branding as lacking knowledge, because people do forget history and history has always repeated itself.

History is like the Japanese art concept of notan: light and dark. History is good and evil; it comes and goes; it is ying and yang; it's now and then. Memory of history is, hurtfully, here and gone. If we recall enough history, we may gain just enough wisdom to maintain balance. Politics is, without doubt, the main stream of history.

Political judgments demand historical knowledge.

Sageisms:

"The men American people admire most extravagantly are the most daring liars; the men they detest most violently are those who try and tell them the truth." -H. L. Mencken

"No man is fit to be a Senator...unless he is willing to surrender his political life for great principle." -Senator Henry Fountain Ashurst

"It is dangerous to be right when the government is wrong." -Voltaire

Chapter Eighteen
Cosmetic Conservatives

"Conservative" is defined as tending to conserve, tending to preserve established institutions, opposed to change, moderate, cautious, etc. Are frugality and practicality lost conservative values?

With only a scant knowledge of history and a heavy dose of party line salted with uninformed logic, a typical CosCon of today seemingly wants to change our basic system. With their solemn, often painted faces and myriad expensive toys, they observe that the government is too big and cumbersome and that they pay way too much in tax.

They want to de-regulate and privatize. They say that they want to change things back to the way they were before. Of course, they want to go back without giving up any of the progress made over the last 100 years. They have become cosmetic conservatives because of their lack of historical knowledge, and their unwitting support of government by the elite. They also make the mistake of confusing our business system with *"Laissez-faire"* capitalism. When markets are dominated by a small number of enormous corporations, it is most definitely not a *"free"* market.

We have witnessed, over the last century, the biggest bust and the greatest prosperity and growth ever known to mankind. We had depressions in 1907 and the 1930's followed by the best 70 years known to mankind.

Depressions:

The short time frame between depressions is highly significant.

1837 to 1843, a sharp downturn in the American economy caused by bank failures and lack of confidence in the paper currency. (In the early 1800's, most corporations were non-profit organizations; the for-profit corporations were usually banks.)

1873 to 1896 - The Long Depression - economic problems in Europe prompt the failure of Jay Cooke & Company, the largest bank in the U.S., bursting the post-Civil War speculative bubble.

Panic of 1907 - A run on Knickerbocker Trust Company in October, 1907 sets events in motion that led to a depression in the United States. The resulting U.S. bank panic was exacerbated by the unstable financial system that allowed highly questionable financial speculation by unscrupulous businessmen.

81

Who'$ Driving?

1929 to late 1930's - The Great Depression – overproduction in the United States, the stock market crash, and a banking collapse sparked a global downturn, including a second downturn in 1937. Mostly forgotten is that the Public Utility stocks (the Dot-Coms of the time) began to crash weeks before the general market. Their decline triggered margin calls forcing further sales of their and then other stocks.

The real economic causes of the Great Depression were declines in employment during periods of capital accumulation combined with increases in production which destabilized the economy. When production is increasing without the expansion of labor's purchasing power, capital enters a period of disaccumulation. The concentration of wealth in the 1920's, eliminated competition and allowed price fixing without the necessary concurrent expansion in employment creating greater demand for goods. Increasing inventories would usually lower prices and increase demand so the artificially high prices contributed greatly to the Great Depression.

Some CosCon economists try to blame the depression on government interference with business. They cite the loose monetary policy of the Federal Reserve in the mid 1920's expanding the money supply as their basis. There is no question this policy allowed greater stock speculation because of the availability of plentiful money in the banking system. Forgotten is that the policy board of the Federal Reserve at the time was dominated by New York bankers who wanted the loose money policy for the benefit of their private banks. The Republican government was in agreement.

Japanese depression - 1991 to present, collapse of a real estate bubble and near collapse of the banking system along with other and more fundamental problems halts Japan's once astronomical growth Only quick and sustained government interference and financial support saved their system from total collapse. This depression is cited only to emphasize the danger inherent in enormous banks.

The common thread in all depressions is that they all were brought on by the mistakes and excesses of the Rich and Powerful and usually by banks. There are two great lessons to be learned from this economic history – make very sure that the mistakes made by the RAP will have only minor consequences and watch the banks. They will make mistakes. They always have! It is the history of the world –all of the economic disasters and much misery.

New Deal reform legislation sets the stage for unprecedented prosperity by limiting the control of the RAP, closer bank regulation and

82

deposit insurance, and through public works programs like the Interstate Highway System and NASA. The last 70 years have been so good that future history should remember it as the *"Great Prosperity."*

To argue that this fantastic prosperity was the result of the New Deal controls is pointless. To argue that it occurred only in spite of the controls ignores its unprecedented length. Neither can be proven. However, it is reasonable to attribute the absence of a depression over that long time frame to just those controls which allowed the impact of the expanding middle class to dominate and grow our economy.

One might argue that Supply-Side economics kept it going. There is no way of knowing that and many, if not most, economic theorists will dispute it. The bursting of the Dot.Com bubble on March 10, 2000 had all the earmarks of a crash before depression. Since that has not happened as yet, most economists concluded that it is and has been the spending habits of the middle class fueling and maintaining the *"Great Prosperity."* For certain, Supply-Side's deficits are not frugal and many believe them to be immoral.

President Ronald Regan is the inspiration of the CosCons. It is his rhetoric that they regurgitate and his programs that they admire. They ignore his warnings. Not all his programs worked well. His tax cuts, and those later ones by the younger Bush, did nothing more than make the rich richer and increase the relative tax burden of the middle class, including many CosCons and moderates.

The reasonableness of Supply-Side thinking, like so many other economic theories, has been discredited in actual practice. You can put more money in the hands of investors, but it does not guarantee creation of jobs or even economic growth. We have twenty-four years since his reform to test their effect.

The concentration of wealth and political power in few hands is reaching a point – the last comparable concentration was the 1920's – where we must now proceed with great caution. Any untoward event could tip the balance toward depression and possibly suspension of our Constitutional rights. We must take nothing for granted.

There was an income tax enacted in 1894, but it was declared unconstitutional by the U.S. Supreme Court a few months later. Public support for such a tax developed and in 1909, President William Howard Taft proposed that the states consider amending the Constitution.

Progressive citizens favored the tax as they were concerned by the growing concentration of wealth in few hands. Some conservatives felt it was needed to finance national emergencies.

Who'$ Driving?

The Sixteenth Amendment was ratified in 1913 creating the *"personal income tax"* with a rate of 1% for income over $3,000 ($4,000 for married couples) rising to a maximum of 7% for $500,000 of income or more. Until recently, both major parties have accepted the idea of a progressive tax on individual income.

Tax rates rose to a top rate of 77% during World War I, fell back during the Roaring Twenties, and rose again during the Great Depression. During World War II, the top rate was as high as 91% and a tax withholding system was enacted – the yield doubled the first year of withholding. It is interesting that President Roosevelt opposed this bill as discriminatory against low and medium income citizens. It became law without his signature. Exemptions were lowered and the base broadened. What had been a tax primarily of high income people became a mass tax. In 1939, there were 4 million income tax returns filed. In 1945, there were 45 million.

There were some small reductions in rates before the Korean War. In the 1960s and 1970s, Congress enacted laws which increased the progressiveness of the income tax. The purpose was to achieve *"equality of sacrifice" and balance.*

The concept that the wealthy should be taxed according to the ability to pay is generally accepted. In recent years, conservative economists and the RAP have appealed to our belief in *"Laissez-faire"* capitalism that the general welfare is best served when the richest are encouraged to save and invest. This is part of the inalienable political fabrications disguised behind our belief in *"Laissez-faire."*

Taxation as the province of the government is political and subject to the democratic processes. Fairness is subjective at best. How can anyone be sure they are paying too much? To remind the British Parliament of this, Edmund Burke in a famous speech about taxation, *"to tax and to please, no more than to love and be wise, is not given to men."*

In 1982, the top tax rate was lowered to 50% as a result of Supply-Side economic thinking. Further cuts came in 1987 to 38.5% and in 1988 to 28% before being raised back to 31% under the elder Bush in 1991 (Gulf War tax.) More raises came in 1993 (35.3%) and 1994 (39.6%) before George W. Bush dropped rates to a top of 35%.

The next few pages contain charts depicting the net effect on our economy of Supply-Side tax cuts and the concentration of wealth due to a loss of income share by the bottom 80% of our American households.

The net effect of the tax cuts since Supply-Side economics introduced the 50% top rate was to make the rich richer. There is no other discernible result. **In the 24 years since Regan lowered rates, the Gross National Product in the US shows an average annual growth rate of 5.93%%. In the 24 years preceding those cuts, the GNP had an annual average growth rate of 8.31%. That is 28.6% slower growth after Supply-Side economics went into effect.**

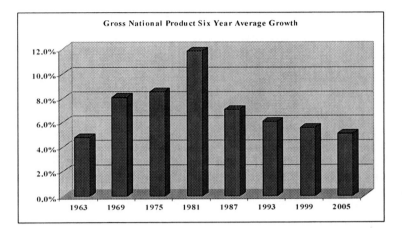

When adjusted for inflation, the results are less startling. In the 24 years since Supply-Side economics lowered rates, the Gross National Product in the US shows an average annual growth rate of 3.12%. In the 24 years preceding those cuts, the GNP had an annual average growth rate of 3.54% - the growth rate before Reagan was 13% faster.

From 1929 to 1976 (47 years of steeply graduated tax rates), the share of the total wealth held by the top 1% of all households declined from 44.2% to 19.9% and our economy grew its fastest. Beginning with Supply-Side economics, the top 1%'s share has climbed back to 39.8% while economic growth slowed (29 years.)

A recent Merrill Lynch report on world wealth shows that America had a 10% increase in the number of millionaires in 2004 to 2.7 million. So, how is that our GNP grew by 3.23% while our millionaires ballooned by 10%? Their growth in numbers should parallel economic growth. There can be no doubt that the concentration of wealth is accelerating as is the political power of the very wealthy and the huge corporations. Plutarch said: *"An imbalance between rich and poor is the oldest and most fatal ailment of all republics."* The greatest threat to liberty lies in the imbalance found in concentration of wealth in few hands

Who'$ Driving?

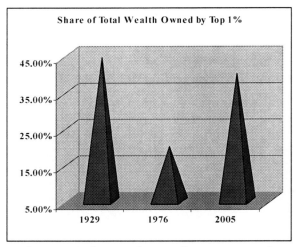

Because the two charts above show contrasting trends, the conclusion must be that the American consumer, as the driving force, is the key - expand the middle class and America expands. By putting more wealth in the hands of more people, everybody gains wealth at a greater rate. In a time frame where most consider government interference to be at its worst and under the most onerous graduated income tax rates, the GNP averaged a real annual growth rate almost 13% greater than under the influence of Supply-Side economics.

What the moderates don't realize is that the tax burden that Reagan and Bush lifted from the RAP was handed mostly to none other than the great middle class. We all know that we pay too much in taxes, but the middle class should be laying blame on our Nonservative leaders.

Below is the tale of the real transfer of tax burden. These figures are from the U.S. Census Bureau Current Population Survey covering the years 1967 to 2001. During that time frame, the household shares of aggregate income – monthly income before taxes and not including lump sum payments or capital gains – shows a distinct shift from the lower levels to the top level. The following six charts display the change in **income share** of American households for those years. Declines for the lowest 80% from 1967 to 1985 resulted from high inflation.

For those households of the lowest fifth (first 20% of households' income distribution,) their share of aggregate income held level at 4.0% of the total from 1967 to 1985. After 1985 (Supply-Side in effect) their share dropped to 3.5% of the total aggregate income by 2001. That's a 15% decrease in their share of household income.

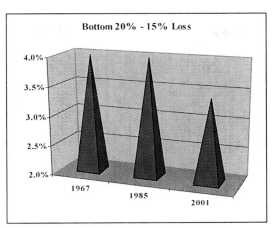

For the next tier (20 to 40%) of households, their income share dropped from 10.8% in 1967 to 9.7% in 1985 as wages did not keep up with inflating prices. It dropped to only 8.7% in 2001 – a 19.4% loss in share. These taxpayers are hard working lower middle class consumers.

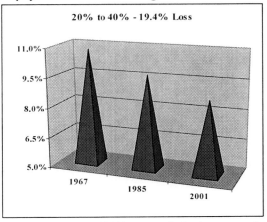

The middle tier (40 to 60%) saw their income share drop from 17.3% in 1967 to 16.3% in 1985 and then to 14.6% in 2001. This was a 15.6% loss of share. These are overspending, middle class consumers.

It is clear that the lowest 60% of households lost a significant portion of their share of national income. This loss is not just the result of changes in relative tax burden, it also reflects downsizing, outsourcing and other managerial policies designed to save money at the expense of lower level employees. These policies also resulted in huge increases in the incomes of corporate management relative to corporate profits.

Who'$ Driving?

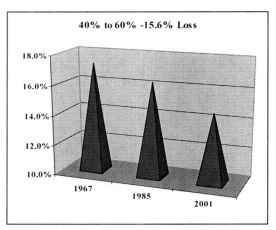

The fourth tier (60 to 80%) actually gained modestly from 1967 to 1985 (24.2% rose to 24.6%) but then fell to 23.0% by 2001. More hard working middle class consumers deprived of income share by 5% through flawed economic policies limiting their frugality and curtailing consumption.

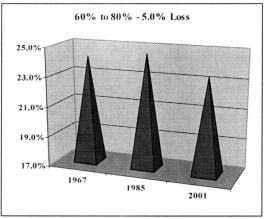

The lower 80% of all American households saw their percentage share of aggregate income decline since the implementation of the "Supply-Side" tax cuts. In 1968, the national minimum wage was $1.60 and in 2005 it was $5.15. The $1.60 of 1968 would purchase $9.12 worth of goods in 2005 dollars. This adds to the welfare burden and is concrete evidence of the futility of Supply-Side economic theory.

The top 20% (80 to 100%) received double benefits. First they are among the prime beneficiaries of our enormous Federal pork barrel, and second they got big tax cuts. Their share rose from 43.8% in 1967 to 45.3% in 1985 and then jumped to 50.1% in 2001. That is a 14.4% gain.

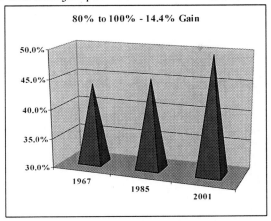

Consider the top 5% of our households whose share fell modestly from 1967 to 1985 (17.5% dropped to 17.0% perhaps due to the oil embargo) and then skyrocketed up to 22.4% in 2001. That 28% gain in their share is the result primarily of Supply-Side economics. High income taxpayers realize the heavy majority of capital gains income: nearly 75% go to taxpayers with household income over $100,000 per year and one-third of that goes to those households with income of $1 million or more. The figures and charts above would show much more bias toward the wealthiest families if capital gain earning were included.

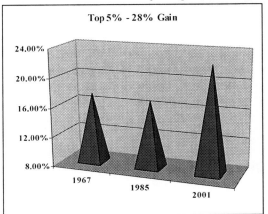

The top 20% of our households earn more than half the total household income, and the top 5% earn almost one-quarter. These are the people with the most political clout. If you consider only the last four years, the relative tax burden among the classes has been shifted to the decided benefit of the top 20% of all households. The relative tax burden of the lowest 40% also declined but not to the extent of the top 20% in actual dollars saved, and it was the second 40% who picked up the burden. These are mostly America's Proservatives.

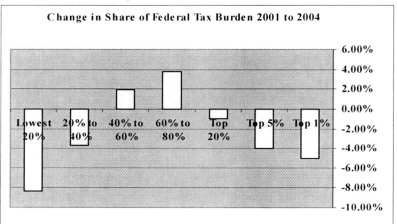

CosCons argue that Supply Side economics was about job creation and not about economic growth. In the 23 years from 1959 to 1982, the number of civilian jobs in the United States grew from 65,341,000 to 99,032,000. That is a rate of 2.24% growth per year. In the 23 year period from 1982 to 2005, the number of jobs grew from 99,032,000 to 142,779,000. That is a growth rate of only 1.84% per year. The rate of growth for 1959 to 1982 is 16.7% more than the rate of growth for 1982 to 2005.

These numbers are skewed significantly in favor of the earlier period since the growth in the labor force also slowed. However, that is offset by the number of unemployed. In 1959 the unemployment rate was 5.9%, in 1982 it was 9.2% and in 2005 it was 4.9%. The higher rate of growth of employment from 1959 to 1982 occurred while unemployment was rising. The lower growth rate from 1982 to 2005 occurred while unemployment was falling. We did not experience the expected greater growth rate during periods of falling unemployment.

If you adjust the data for all three dates using a 6% unemployment rate, the growth in employment from 1959 to 1982 averaged 2.53% per year while the growth rate from 1982 to 2005 averaged only 1.64% per year. These numbers almost exactly match the growth rate in the labor force for the two periods. The conclusion must be that the period of Supply Side economics had neither an advantage nor a disadvantage over the previous period from the standpoint of job creation. In effect, we made the rich richer without the significant job increases promised.

If you examine the rate of capital investment in new plants and equipment for the periods before and after the Supply-Side programs were enacted, you will find a similar equality. It would seem that putting more wealth in the hands of those expected to invest and create jobs did not induce them to increase their rate of investment. The utilization of capital investment in terms of percent of capacity before (81.85%) and after (80.81%) the introduction of Supply-Side programs displays more favorable investment results in the earlier period.

In addition the tax burden born by corporate America has declined significantly. In 1956, corporations paid 28% of our nation's total tax revenues. For fiscal 2004, corporations paid only 11.4%. How much of this is due to unpatriotic tax evasion schemes? According to a report issued by Citizens for Tax Justice, the top ten recipients of corporate tax breaks from 2001 to 2003 were GM, SBC Communications, Citigroup, IBM, Microsoft, AT&T, ExxonMobile, Verizon, J.P. Morgan, Chase and Pfizer. This is welfare for some extremely rich *"persons."*

Looking at the *"Great Prosperity"* as a whole, there is a decided correlation between a steeply graduated income tax and the mobility of individuals among the classes. The New Deal and other progressive programs encouraged a broadening of income down through the social classes. There can be no other explanation for the greater prosperity and growth during past periods of high tax rates combined with excessive governmental interference in the business world. The ambitious members of the lower classes have greater opportunity to invent and innovate and we all benefit under those conditions.

Three of our wealthiest, who apparently know history, have warned about this economic imbalance. The effect on economic mobility – movement from one income group to another over a lifetime – has been negative. Some recent studies indicate it has declined over the last two decades. Alan Greenspan said: *"For the democratic society, that is not a very desirable thing to allow it to happen."* The current trends can turn a meritocracy into an aristocracy since wealth ends in the hands of inheritors rather than in the hands of the gifted and energetic.

Warren Buffet, like Andrew Carnegie, has stated opposition to the transfer of great fortunes from one generation to the next. Mahatma Gandhi said: *"The things that will destroy us are: politics without* *principle; pleasure without conscience; **wealth without work**; knowledge without character; business without morality; science without humanity; and worship without sacrifice.*"

Most Americans agree there should be some relationship between ability to pay and individual tax burdens - *"equality of sacrifice."* Those with the large income are the most fortunate beneficiaries of the greatest economic and political system devised by mankind. Surely they deserve what they earn, but they need to give back as well, and they can and should carry a greater burden of taxation. If they value their progeny, they will even agree to that concept. **They need to recognize that our standards providing their opportunity to excel must have balance to be maintained.** That balance is all important and demands that they contribute on an "equality of sacrifice" basis. Shouldn't our limo be a Ford frugally running on ethanol? Who's driving?

Sageisms:

"The difference between a politician and a statesman is: a politician thinks of the next election and a statesman thinks of the next generation." -James Freeman Clarke

"Read no history: nothing but biography, for that is life without theory." -Benjamin Disraeli

"'My country, right or wrong' is a thing no patriot would ever think of saying except in a desperate case. It is like saying 'My mother, drunk or sober.'" -G. K. Chesterton

"It is at the bottom of life we must begin, not at the top." -Booker T. Washington

"Whatever you are, be a good one." -Abraham Lincoln

"Each party steals so many articles of faith from the other, and the candidates spend so much time making each other's speeches, that by the time election day is past there is nothing much to do save turn the sitting rascals out and let a new gang in." -H. L. Mencken

"All the world over, I will back the masses against the classes." -William Ewart Gladstone

Chapter Nineteen
Powered by Ford

Henry Ford (1863-1947)

Henry Ford opened the Ford Motor Car Company on an initial investment of $28,000 in 1903 with eleven other investors. The billions of dollars earned and reinvested by his company since then all came from the consuming public.

At the dawn of the automobile age, Henry Ford predicted that *"ethyl alcohol is the fuel of the future"* and his first car was made to run on ethanol. During World War II, the U.S., Brazil and other nations relied on ethanol to extend gasoline supplies. In the postwar period, however, gasoline was so plentiful and cheap that ethanol lost its allure. Ethanol is also safer as it burns slowly and does not explode like gasoline.

Ask yourself why the United States has not aggressively pursued alternate fuels in the past 30 years. Then ask your self who is spending the most money lobbying Congress. If you don't see a connection, you must want to believe in corporations and your conservative leadership so greatly that you are neither practical nor frugal and definitely not conservative. Corporations can and do stifle invention and innovation.

When the first oil embargo struck in 1972, Brazil undertook steps to develop ethanol as an alternate fuel source and now a significant percentage of their fuel consumption is ethanol. Here in America it is insignificant. Could we have done that? We have and can accomplish virtually anything we set our minds to. Why didn't we set out minds to alternate fuels? The answer is simply the oil industry does not want an alternate fuel and they have the ears of our Nonservatives.

In 1914, Henry Ford doubled the daily wage of most of his workers. This unusual move gave this frugal man's employees more purchasing power and their increased spending stimulated consumption elsewhere. It outraged most other employers but was a significant event in expanding the consuming middle class. It may have been one of Ford's best investments since it raised the standard of living for most workers and increased national consumption. They could then afford his cars.

A commonly accepted definition, in today's political world, of a *"liberal"* is one who advocates taking from the rich to give to the poor. In today's political world a practical definition of a *"conservative"* is one who advocates taking from the lower 80% of households to further enrich the aristocratic top 20%.

This definition of a *"conservative"* was equally applicable to all of history prior to the Twentieth Century - the ancient world, the feudalistic Middle Ages, and even the early centuries of the industrial revolution. Those systems never saw the enormous expansion of the middle class that has so enriched the world in the last 100 years, and they were all essentially failures as social systems. Even the early centuries of the industrial revolution were, more or less, failures due to numerous and frequent depressions that devastated so many. A practical observation is that those systems were inferior and the practical *"equality of sacrifice"* system of taxation yields superior results.

Can we measure the damage done in our system by taking from the poor to give to the rich? We can use our experience in comparative household income from 1977 to 1999 to make such a measure. The comparison is of after-tax income using the same percentage shares of after tax income experienced in 1977 applied to 1999 after tax income:

The lowest fifth of all households have average income of $8,800 in 1999; it was $7,300 in 1977. If they had maintained an equal percentage share to that they held in 1977, their household income would have been $12,100. Because they lost percentage share of after tax income to higher income households, they lost $3,300 in average income. That is a 27% loss in their share and an even greater loss in their consumption.

The second fifth lost $3,700; the middle fifth lost $3,500; and the fourth fifth lost $3,400. These losses combined gave the top fifth a $13,900 increase in average household after tax income. The top 1% of all households experienced a gain of about $225,000 per household. A significant part of the losses for the middle 60% was their higher tax burden and part of the gain of the top 20% was their lower taxes!

The bottom 80% of our earning households lost about $3475 per year each in average household income. These are mostly hardworking consumers who deserve better treatment from whomever it is that is driving. They are also the voters and they should be driving.

What effect on our economy would have been seen if this transfer upward of percentage income share had not occurred?

Who'$ Driving?

Consumer spending accounts for about 66% of our Gross National Product. Using the statistics comparing income and expenditures for 1999, if you take back the $13,900 gain in share by the top 20% of households and return to the first 80% of our households the $3,475 of average household income each lost due to their declining shares from 1977 to 1999, their increased expenditures would far exceed the calculated decrease in expenditures by the top 20%.

The top 20% of households will spend only about 70% of the $13,900 they gained, whereas the bottom 80% would have spent virtually all of that $13,900 if they had only maintained their household share of 1977. If this percentage share transfer upward had not occurred, the 1999 Gross National Product would have been $1.1 trillion greater. **That would have represented a 13% gain for our Gross National Product for the single year 1999.**

This is why our economy grew at a greater rate prior to the supply-side tax cuts than after. The income of the much greatest number of middle class consumers was growing at a greater rate as was their consumption expenditures. **Consumption, not investment and production, is the key to growth. Balance not only protects the integrity of our system, it creates greater potential for prosperity.**

These numbers are slightly skewed since the lowest 20% of families spend much more than their income. It should also be noted that the bottom 20% contains large numbers of those under 25 years of age (using credit, student loans and welfare) and those over 65 using savings, Medicare and Medicaid. If you drop out the bottom 20%, the national net expenditures gain would still have been more than $600 billion - a 7% gain for our GNP in 1999. The consumer is the key to economic prosperity, because of the large numbers involved.

Those are significant gains and that is only for one year. If you compound the gains over the span of years of the Great Prosperity, it becomes the Greatest Prosperity. There can be little doubt that over time the income theoretically given up by the top 20% would have returned to them compounded again and again. This group with large discretionary spending choices often makes expenditures that will not add directly to the economy. The purchase of fine arts, antiques and other collectables (over $2 million for one car) only pushes the value of such items higher. These are not the kinds of investments that will grow an economy.

When you have large numbers of people earning decent wages, you have large and growing consumption and savings. This is the biggest difference between the developed nations and the low income nations.

Who'$ Driving?

Of the world's 6 billion people, more than 1.2 billion live on less than $1 a day. Two billion more people are only marginally better off. You can't build an economy based on the people spending less than $1 a day.

Aristotle said: *"The most perfect political community is one in which the middle class is in control, and outnumbers both of the other classes."* This is also true in the economic community as well. Government and corporate policy should pursue programs that will put more income in the hands of the spenders because money spent multiplies again and again. Henry Ford proved this and left a legacy on the world with his inventions and innovations. The creation of national franchise dealers was a precedent that has been copied over and over. Assembly line manufacturing allowed Detroit and then America to make enough. Doubling his employees' wages places him on a list of eminence with few others.

It is incredible stupid to pursue government policies allowing the relative share of household income of the middle class to decline while increasing their relative tax burden. Eventually, it should lead to a major depression. You could call it **Consumer-Side Economics** since the expansion and empowerment of the middle class made our entire nation richer. Consumption by many is the most efficient engine driving any economy, and rich and poor alike prosper most under conditions of liberty, free trade and stable political conditions, driven by *"We the People"* and for all practicality powered by Henry Ford's frugal legacy.

Sageisms:

"There is one safeguard known generally to the wise, which is an advantage and security to all, but especially to democracies as against despots. What is it? Distrust!" -Demosthenes

"Politics: the art of keeping as many balls as possible up in the air at one time -- while protecting your own." - Sam Attlesey

"Independence I have long considered as the grand blessing of life, the basis of every virtue; and independence I will ever secure by contracting my wants, though I were to live on a barren heath."
-Mary Wollstonecraft

"Few men have virtue enough to withstand the highest bidder."
-George Washington

Who'$ Driving?

Chapter Twenty
Deficit Dilemma

In 2001, the total net worth of all households in the United States was over $42.4 trillion. Around $29 trillion (about 70%) was held by only 10% of the population. About $11.4 trillion (27%) was held by the next 40%. Less than $2 trillion was held by the bottom 50% of the population. With an estimated population of 277.8 million, the top 10% had a net worth of almost $10.8 million each. The next 40% held around $102,600 each. The bottom 50% had a net worth of less than $9,400 each. Sizable numbers of people had a negative net worth.

One can applaud and admire the gains of the innovators at the top, but one must also be concerned with the losses of the middle and bottom. Often the ones at the top are not the innovators but their children – of our top 15 billionaires, the fortunes of eight was inherited. In one calendar year, the total net worth of the Forbes 500 increased from $738 billion to over one trillion dollars. The average increase per person was $655 million. That is about $75,000 per hour (all hours in a year) after all taxes and all expenses.

These are unsustainable trends. It has nothing to do with fairness; it has to do with the lessons of history. We have forgotten the violence of the labor movement of the 1920's and 1930's where company paid thugs was used to intimidate workers. We have forgotten the torching of our cities in the 1960's by our lowest classes. The government sent in the army reserves to restore order. We have forgotten that the *"war on poverty"* was born of this violence. While that war was ill-advised and self-defeating, the threat to property was real and the reaction of the rich and powerful was predictable.

It is not the inequities that are dangerous in and of themselves; it is the inequities combined with the great political power derived from the concentration of wealth. Plutarch said: *"An imbalance between rich and poor is the oldest and most fatal ailment of all republics."* When Reagan took office, the Federal Debt was $909 billion. When the elder President Bush left office, twelve years later, it had ballooned to $4,202 billion.

Supply-Side economics must mean the lowest *"Eighty"* (80%) are here mostly to consume thereby supplying the top *"Twenty"* (20%) with more riches, and we are working harder for less after-tax income.

The typical American household in 1998 worked about 60 hours per week –the highest rate in the world and accumulated virtually no savings. We work 350 hours more a year than workers in Europe – nine weeks.

Who'$ Driving?

Toward the end of President Clinton's tenure, the government was running budget surpluses. Although many had warned about deficits, President Bush decided the surpluses belonged to the richest taxpayers and that tax cuts would stimulate the economy and there would be no deficits. He was half right as lower taxes encouraged greater consumer spending and the economy has improved with higher employment rates. He was terrible wrong about the deficits. **Deficits violate our value of frugality and are patently immoral passing our debts down to future generations.**

Three tax cuts and two wars later, we have record deficits of $375 billion in 2003 (3.5% of our national income,) $412 billion in 2004 and $427 billion in 2005. Further deficits are expected through 2008 at a rate of at least 2% of our national income. We are now over $8.6 trillion in total national debt - add half a billion while you read this book. That is almost $29,000 for each of us. For more than 50% of the households in the country, that is equal to about triple their total net worth. That lowest 50% have little chance to be frugal.

When the baby-boom generation reaches retirement collecting Social Security and Medicare, the deficit will see further increases. Saving rates in America have always been among the lowest in the world and the deficit is eating up 33% of those savings. Another significant part of those savings are necessary just to replace obsolete equipment, factories and housing. When sufficient savings are not available to finance new plants and equipment, the economy will stagnate.

That is exactly what happened when the deficit averaged 4.2% of out national income in the 1980's under Reagan. Net new investment in plants and equipment declined to the lowest level since the 1940's and real wages turned flat. This necessitated massive borrowings from abroad. We were already running large trade deficits so the imbalance is setting new records. Much of the record corporate profits are being invested overseas.

The negative side of large trade deficits and debt imbalance is the political pressure from lobbyists wanting protectionist measures. This, in turn, raises the prices consumers must pay; which, in turn, reduce their saving rate; which, in turn, increases the percentage of savings consumed by the deficit; which, in turn, increases our borrowing from abroad; which, in turn, increases the debt imbalance; which, in turn, increases political pressure from lobbyists wanting protectionist measures, which, in turn, … a dangerous circuity violating frugal and moderate values. Many consider it immoral as well. It is certainly not balanced.

Who'$ Driving?

The argument that tax cuts will promote investment and economic growth ignores actual experience. The gains, if any, based on the tax cuts are jeopardized by the detriments experienced from large deficits. All of which is complicated further by the inflation rate. Understand when a person has a net worth in six figures or higher, inflation generally works in that person's favor by increasing the value of investments. If your net worth is less, inflation curtails real consumption.

Starting with the oil embargo in the early 1970's and largely because of steep inflation, median family income in America was virtually stagnant until the early 1990's. Now, we have had another oil crisis raising fuel prices significantly. Are we looking forward to another decade of more of income stagnation? Is there any possibility it may be worse than stagflation; could it degenerate into a severe recession or even a depression? We may not now have serious problems here, but it is best to be prepared.

As our nation gained wealth and security over the Great Prosperity, we became more tolerant and giving. The *"war on poverty"* was embraced. It is now the subject of great contention only because it was botched. The solution to poverty is education and job opportunity not hand outs. When income stagnated in the 1980's and early 1990's, we saw a rise in domestic terrorism which may reflect a less tolerant society.

Because the basic character of our society may be changing for the worse, our Christian segment seems to be more demanding of adherence to their beliefs and moral values. Our attitude toward illegal and even legal immigrants has hardened. Democracy must, by its very nature, be tolerant since it is a coalition of many diverse groups. We have become defensive to the point where many seem willing to give up basic liberties because of a fear fanned by a political slogan. Deficit financing, no matter the rationale, is not just economically dangerous, it threatens the civility of our society. Is the rising crime rate directly connected to falling income shares at the lowest levels?

To anticipate that deficit financing will stimulate sufficient growth to wipe out the deficit ignores our experience of the last 25 years. Tax increases are widely disliked, but those under the elder Bush and Clinton helped close the deficit and apparently did not hurt the recovering economy. Spending cuts under Clinton were mostly military and were augmented by domestic program cuts under the Republican majority starting in 1995, thanks to some frugality in Newt Gingrich's *"Contract with America."* They are incumbents now and their priorities have changed – proving that incumbency tends toward liberalism.

Who'$ Driving?

Spending cuts by the present administration are virtually non-existent. They are listening to the lobbyists and implementing their demands. The military costs can not be touched. The only viable solution is tax increases. Since the *"Supply-Side"* tax cuts have proven counterproductive, it would seem best to put the highly graduated income tax back in place. As a practical matter, we did have the best of the *"Great Prosperity"* under that system of taxes.

All administrations over the last 53 years have added significantly to the nation's debt. Eisenhower took office with the National Debt around $275 billion. Most of this debt had been incurred during the Civil War, the First World War, the Great Depression and World War II. At present the National Debt is almost $8.4 trillion more than that.

Our Nonservative Republican administrations have added $6,430 billion in the last 33 years they occupied the White House, significantly more than the spendthrift Nonservative Democrats added - $1,955 billion in their last 20 years. The Republicans share represents an average gain of $194.9 billion per year. Democrats have added $80.5 billion on average per year.

If you take Eisenhower's, Nixon's and Ford's $428 billion addition over their 16 years ($26.75 billion per year) out of the above equation, Supply-Side Republicans have added over $6 trillion to our national debt - representing a rate of $300 billion per year – about 3.75 times greater per year than the Democratic administrations. Reagan's farewell: *"I've been asked if I have any regrets. Well, I do. The deficit is one."*

Our 2006 national budget of over $2.77 trillion will add almost another $400 billion to our National Debt. The interest in 2006 alone on the debt will exceed $350 billion. That is almost 14% of the total budget by itself, almost 90% of this year's deficit itself, and will come very close to exceeding the total of the national debt when Nixon was elected. Over one-half of the national budget is payments to individuals – the Federal payroll and retirement costs. Benefits are additional.

It is estimated that by 2040, total federal revenues will not cover interest on the national debt. We could just ignore this problem. Economic theory says it will be solved naturally. That solution will come in the form of devastating inflation or a world wide depression wiping out most economies and their debts, or both.

It should seem evident that our Nonservative administrations have interests other than frugality and reducing the size of our government by balancing the budget. We are immorally building a debt that our children will eventually have to pay. We should try to make sure that they pay on an *"equality of sacrifice"* basis since our budget deficits reflect the significant tax breaks given to those in the highest earning households and reflect the wasteful spending programs that benefit most those in our highest earning households. Our huge budget deficits also reflect the deception of our Nonservative administrations when they claim allegiance to the conservative values of smaller and more efficient government. It is positive proof of inalienable political fabrications.

Should all of us be concerned, including the aristocracy? Absolutely! The field of inequities needs to be leveled out – **greater balance in our inequities.** Those at the top need to remember who it is that shoulders the greatest hardships in wars protecting their assets; needs to remember where they came from; and needs to remember that we Americans are all in this together. Even more, they need to recognize that **the American consumer is the key to both economic prosperity and political security.** Over and over the Nonservative leadership mouth allegiance to smaller government, tax cuts and deregulation. Their record confirms otherwise. They talk the talk but don't walk the walk. Current trends are not moral, practical or frugal.

Ask who it was that raised our moral and ethical standards. Ask who it was who invented and innovated. Even before the wide spread of education, it was always the thinkers and strivers, mostly common men – see confirmation in *"Liberty in the New Millennium,"* the last chapter in *"The Triumph of Liberty"* by Jim Powell.

A true conservative, with a foundation of historical knowledge, would look at the state of the world today and observe that we never had it so good materially. We could have had it better through increased consumption based on *"equality of sacrifice"* system of taxation and on real competition in the business world. That will not be accomplished by allowing huge corporations to buy up their competition. You can stop this trend toward consolidation through government interference utilizing the anti-trust laws and highly graduated corporate taxes. Any argument that things could have been better without the government interference is pure speculation and ignores the lessons of economic cycles.

Before the Great Depression, the small businessman was only slightly better off than the working class. The middle class was made up of the larger farmers, professionals, small manufactures, some skilled tradesmen, and merchants. Their numbers were not great compared to the total population. The New Deal did help change that. Programs such as FHA/VA loan guarantees allowed common folk to purchase basic housing. The legal foundations for retirement programs provided another means for little people to save money before taxes. A steep graduated tax system (up to 91%) helped to redistribute the wealth down the social structure.

Prior to the Great Depression, the terms required to purchase your own home were a barrier to all except the most well off. The minimum down payment required was one-third of the sales price, but fifty percent was common. The mortgage usually had to be paid within five to seven years. In recent years, home ownership has become one of the great stabilizers in our economy.

The rise of labor unions aided the process of wealth redistribution. Common man united to compel the rich and powerful to spread the wealth. The minimum wage laws and unemployment compensation programs contributed to this process. While there is little question that the labor unions went too far, there was never a union contract not also approved and signed by management, so they, also, bear responsibility for the excesses. In the process, many, if not most, of the union workers were elevated into the middle class. (Democracy and *"Laissez-faire"* economics allow people to band together for selfish objectives. Our Revolution was just that, and that is also what corporations are.)

We have seen an enormous expansion and enrichment of the middle class, which now powers America and the world. It is not giant industry; it is the purchasing power and spending habits of the middle class that have fueled the unbelievable economic growth and prosperity we have seen over the last 70 years. To continue this fabulous growth, we need to maximize consumption by the many. Who's driving?

Sageisms:

"Were we directed from Washington when to sow and when to reap we should soon want bread." -Thomas Jefferson

"Politics is the gentle art of getting votes from the poor and campaign funds from the rich by promising to protect each from the other." -Oscar Ameringer

"It is an unfortunate human failing that a full pocketbook often groans more loudly than an empty stomach." -Franklin Delano Roosevelt

"Can any of you seriously say the Bill of Rights could get through Congress today? It wouldn't even get out of committee." -F. Lee Bailey

Who'$ Driving?

Chapter Twenty-one
Revisions not narrow

FROM THE OFFICE OF PUBLIC AFFAIRS

"Treasury Announces Successful Privatization of Sallie Mae
"Treasury officials today completed the formal cutting of all ties of the Student Loan Marketing Association, commonly known as Sallie Mae or SLMA, with the federal government. Documents signed at the Treasury Department this afternoon effectively dissolved Sallie Mae, a government-sponsored enterprise subsidiary of SLM Corporation, completing a process that began in 1996. Today's action completed the transformation of Sallie Mae to a fully private corporation.

"The privatization of Sallie Mae was considered something of an experiment when proposed in 1996," said Treasury Assistant Secretary for Financial Institutions Wayne A. Abernathy, who signed the documents that made the transition final. "I am pleased that we have completed this transformation almost four years ahead of schedule. We applaud the transformation of Sallie Mae into a wholly private company, dynamically increasing its options to provide financing services to students. This is a mission well accomplished."

"Congress originally established Sallie Mae in 1972 as a government-sponsored enterprise (GSE) to help students by facilitating a secondary market in federally guaranteed student loans. As a GSE, it had benefits such as exemptions from state and local taxes, but it was limited in the kinds of business it could enter.

"In 1996, Congress enacted the SLMA Reorganization Act, which began the process of converting Sallie Mae into a private business while still meeting the needs of the borrowing student public. Sallie Mae's shareholders approved a reorganization that created SLM Corporation, a Delaware-chartered holding company, and the Sallie Mae GSE became its wholly-owned subsidiary. This process facilitated a smooth transition for the student loan market, culminating in the GSE's dissolution today. The Sallie Mae privatization included the establishment of a trust, satisfactory to Treasury, defeasing the remaining liabilities of the GSE. The dissolution of SLMA is well ahead of the September 30, 2008 deadline set by Congress.

"The Treasury Department has exercised oversight responsibilities over Sallie Mae, including monitoring its privatization process. The document signed by Assistant Secretary Abernathy today is a formal

recognition, required by the law, that the outstanding obligations of the now-dissolved GSE are sufficiently collateralized."

Sallie-Mae lobbied for changes in the student loan laws because their original intended motive to help disadvantaged students has been corrupted, by privatization, into maximizing profits.

Congress recently passed an increase in allowed interest rates on student loans. Even more recently Congress passed legislation hurting student loan borrowers even more and effectively ending competition in the market place. Student loans usually carry variable interest rates but students and parents could convert these loans to fixed rate consolidation loans without sacrificing the federal guarantee. The lender is guaranteed against loss in either case. Many made these conversions locking in favorably low, fixed interest rates.

The new Bush sponsored budget deficit act provides that **those who have or will consolidate student loans can only refinance one time.** The borrower will be barred from later shopping the loan to other lenders. Ask yourself, how this law fits into *"laissez-faire"* capitalism? From the late 1990s to 2005, Sallie-Mae had an annual rate of total return to investors of 26%. If the public wants to provide affordable financing for education of the less advantaged, you would expect the government loan guarantees to result in a more reasonable rate of corporate profit. **This legislation effectively hurts our children just to benefit banks and that is patently immoral.**

If students cannot refinance for lower rates, more of them will surely default, so they get hurt by the inability to refinance, and taxpayers get hurt because we have guaranteed these loans and have to pay the lender their losses which can never be losses. The default rate on any type of loan is directly related to the level of the interest rate. Thus, the American taxpayer wants students to be able to refinance. *"Laissez-faire"* capitalism says they should have the ability to refinance.

Obviously, any lower rates should cost the government and all taxpayers less money, so who then wants to bar lower rates? It is Sallie Mae and the other big lenders who don't want the lure of lower rates tempting their customers to switch to competitors.

Federal student loan guarantee guidelines allowed the lenders to retain additional profits gained from interest rate increases. When rate declines would cost the lenders interest income, we subsidize the lender that interest. Heads they win, tails you lose; and you are *"We the People."* **America is about the children and not the banks or huge corporations.**

How long will it be before the federal government enacts a limit to just one refinancing of home mortgage loans? Would the American people stand for that? The logic of the student loans, supposedly, was that it would reduce the government's liability on defaulted loans over the long run. Could not the banks lobby for similar, fallacious reductions in the government's liability on federally guaranteed home loans.

Look at the for-profit educational institutions. They solicit the marginal students to better themselves through education. They sign them up, provide the student loans (collecting a commission,) and provide the facilities and personnel to fulfill the agreement. About three-quarters of students at these institutions take out student loans averaging almost $7,000. About 60% of the enrollees graduate and 100% of their loans are paid. The non-profit higher educational institutions also are paid commissions on student loans. The very institutions we entrust with our children to look out for them and provide opportunity for higher education are using our children's needs for financial benefit.

Now, the CosCons applaud the revision of the bankruptcy laws, probably written by the credit card companies which are the banks, making it tougher for the common man who may be bankrupted by ill health or downsizing. Over half the family bankruptcies filed every year in the United States are directly related to medical expenses, and a recent study shows that 75 percent of those are filed by people with health insurance. This change will benefit only the banks. And we now have huge banks only because the *"anti-change"* CosCons approved major changes in public protective banking laws. The struggling young worker cannot use bankruptcy to ease the burden of student loans.

Andrew Jackson, 1867-1845

Under President Jackson in 1835 was the last time there was no national debt. Large banks have been a major political issue since our nation began. Jefferson and Madison opposed them. Andrew Jackson fought against the National Bank, which he considered a dangerous symbol of greed exactly opposing our democratic ideals.

Profits are the mark of corporate success. However, when profits are in

105

part the result of special legislation benefiting particular corporate people, there is something seriously wrong. It is not *"Laissez-faire"* economics; it is *"laissez-unfair"* economics. In 2005, corporate after-tax profits in America, as a proportion of GDP, rose to the highest point since 1930. Over the last few years, corporate profits have risen by 60% while working consumer's income increased only 10%. The banking industry is the most profitable in the nation based upon return on equity.

Part of the increase in corporate profits comes directly from subdued wage growth. The share of national income going to wage and salary workers has fallen under 60% where it normally runs between 64% and 67%. This can be explained, in part, by technological gains providing increased productivity and lower production costs. This is the normal experience during the early stages of technological change; but the extra profits are supposed to fall to increased competition in time. However, when the government interferes with special laws benefiting specific corporations, competition is effectively eliminated – it is not free market.

Both the experience of history and economic theory say that profits should grow at the same rate as the Gross National Product. If they do, and the income of consumers grows at the same relative rate, the economy will continue to prosper. If you artificially introduce an imbalance by special legislation or by allowing an over-concentration of wealth, the economy is jeopardized. True conservatives, believing in "Laissez-faire" capitalism, should oppose the lobbyists system that interferes with capitalism and benefits the rich and politically powerful.

We elect the same congressmen again and again. They tell us the inalienable political fabrications we want to hear; and then they do what those providing their financing tell them to do. We do this without considering the cost to our children who are trying to get started. They are America's future, yet reasonable people stand aside and allow corporate America to exercise their political advantage to the detriment of our children. Eventually the bill will be paid. Unfortunately, history says it could even lead to the loss of liberty. Who's driving?

Sageism:

"It is the nature, and the advantage, of strong people that they can bring out the crucial questions and form a clear opinion about them. The weak always have to decide between alternatives that are not their own."
-Dietrich Bonhoeffer

Who'$ Driving?

Chapter Twenty-two
Neither Frugal nor Practical

Global warming is another contentious issue between LamLibs and CosCons. The LamLibs contend that pollution is having potentially disastrous effects on the environment. CosCons say there is no convincing evidence. No one doubts our air is badly polluted.

Who knows? **However, the incidence of asthma in America is skyrocketing, especially among young children.** They are America's most valuable asset! We should all put aside our differences and demand that Corporate America clean up its act and our air. Many also seem to feel that the unfortunate increase in autism is directly related to pollution. How can the motivation for corporate profits compare with the health of our populace and especially our children? Certainly the standard of the *"General Welfare"* would demand that we clean up the environment.

"The test of the morality of a society is what it does for its children." - Dietrich Bonhoeffer. Are American children second class citizens to corporate *"persons?"*

We are second class citizens in the world when it comes to our medical system and our soft drinks. Why should we be second class in anything? It is because corporate profits come before us and the US. How sweet is sweet, or is it bittersweet?

Home

Mom washed all our clothe in a tub
It was hard work, a rub-a-dub-dub
Our dryer was two rollers with a hand crank
A wringer to squeeze out the water so rank
Our icebox kept food cool just with ice
A hard wood box with brass handles so nice
Milk was delivered right to our home
Sometimes with ice cream to eat in a cone
The bottles were glass with a cardboard stopper
Long before the time of Elvis or the Big Bopper
Soft drinks also came bottled in glass
They were a lot sweeter then, you can bet your ass

Federal interference in the sugar industry dates back to the War of 1812. We bewail government interference in business while businesses and corporations welcome it. In 1934, imposed sugar import quotas were added to the high sugar tariffs and direct government subsidies to growers in order to protect the growers from the vagaries of international pricing. So they set the prices as the growers wanted and it now costs us more than $100,000 per year for each grower.

Sugar quotas were eliminated by Congress in 1974, but reinstated in 1982 under President Reagan. That was supposedly part of a program to cut wasteful spending by taking it out of federal subsidies; but it was accomplished by putting the cost in artificially high prices on the super market shelves so the consumer would directly subsidize the growers. A Commerce Department study estimated that the sugar program costs American consumers more than $3 billion (your share is $10) a year. But it's not all pork anymore – we pay it directly in the price of sugar.

Well, government pro-active meddling backfired when the soft drink industry abandoned sugar as the preferred sweetener and went to high-fructose corn syrup. The result is that we get soft drinks that are not as sweet as in the rest of the world. One of the reasons that corn syrup can compete with sugar is that the corn industry gets $5.5 billion ($16.50 from you) a year in subsidies – about 25% of corn grower's revenue.

Isn't America wonderful? We pay to subsidize an inferior choice to sweeten our soft drinks while artificially supporting the price of the superior choice. Then both choices use our artificial support to hire lobbyists to keep it that way. Canada has cheaper sugar because they have no sugar growers. We should be so lucky, but, then, we have the wrong people driving. Those Nonservatives driving right now are liberal and not frugal or practical. Are they moral?

Harvard did a study that indicated the adolescent boy's consumption of soft drinks from 1991 to 1994 increased by almost 70%. Another study showed that children who drink soda pop regularly tend to be fatter and more likely to develop diabetes later in life than those consuming less soft drink. Fructose may be frugal, but it is not practical and it may be harming our kids.

Interestingly, children in much of the Third World consume large quantities of soft drinks with higher levels of sucrose and they have a lower rate of obesity than American children. Some scientists allege that the fructose in American soft drinks may play a role in stimulating appetite not found in cane sugar used elsewhere in the world.

"One Nation under God" does not apply to the *"persons"* who are our giant multi-national corporations. Our automobile industry has difficulty competing with foreign companies because, in part, our health

care and retirement plans are so much more expensive. Our drug industry offers considerably lower prices in foreign countries. Is this moral? Is it patriotic?

We are told by our high-tech companies to call for their technical support. They don't seem to be concerned with the fact that we can't understand their foreign support personnel because they have already made their sale. Outsourcing may add significantly to the bottom line, but what does it do to the consuming power of our workers? Many large corporations have moved their *"charters"* to foreign nations in order to lower their tax burden. So, who gets their tax burden? Over the long run, these moves must be self-defeating. They are certainly not patriotic.

Our Nonservatives in Washington use the word *"Earmark."* That word has four definitions in the dictionary. As a noun it is either *"a brand put on the ear of livestock"* or *"an identifying mark or feature."* As an intransitive verb, it is either *"to set such a brand or mark on"* or *"to reserve for a special purpose."* Certainly it must be the last definition. American citizens use the word *"pork."* Our Nonservative government put their brand on our middle class ears reserving tax dollars for the sole purpose of further enrichment of the upper classes.

When you pass 6,371 *"earmarks"* in one bill there can no longer be one special purpose other than to liberally satisfy the demands of special interests. *"Earmarks"* now account for only $71.8 billion (20% of the deficit and $240 is your share) of the Federal Budget, which may seem insignificant. Viewed from the standard of true frugal conservatism, any amount is significant. Our system demands that special interests be ignored. It is just the tip of the iceberg, when measured by the waste handed to the RAP in so much more of the budget. We financed a $225 million dollar bridge in Alaska to an island with 50 inhabitants. Nikita Krushchev said: *"Politicians are the same all over. They promise to build a bridge even where there is no river."* In this case, there was water to cross, but it was not frugal, practical or moral.

Sageisms:

"Government is a trust, and the officers of the government are trustees. And both the trust and the trustees are created for the benefit of the people." -Senator Henry Clay

"Power concedes nothing without a demand. It never did and it never will." -Frederick Douglass

Chapter Twenty-three
Health Care Disrepair

From the year 2000 to the year 2004, the American population under 65 years of age increased by 10 million while those covered by employment based medical insurance fell by almost 5 million. Doesn't that seem odd? The corporate aristocracy is cutting employee health benefits to add to the bottom line and their bonuses.

Now the lobbyists are attacking Medicare. The new drug program is so one sided that there must be a strong suspicion that it was written by the drug and insurance industries and then sent to Congress for their rubber stamp. This is a direct result of the imbalance of power in our system. The lobbyists influence on the Washington bureaucracy has gone too far. How is it that a human gene can be patented? These patents surely impede medical research.

A poll in 2005 found only 36 percent of the public thinks the FDA is doing a good job. This is down from 56 percent from a year earlier showing that the moderate public has concerns about the FDA's independence in reaching decisions ensuring safe medications.

There is current evidence that the trend which transferred hospital care from the publicly financed hospitals to the enormous corporate hospital chains has resulted in poorer medical care. At one time, the county and city hospitals were virtually the only centers for medical care. Now, they are in the minority. There is also reason to believe we are not getting the kind of care we are accustomed to and deserve.

According to the journal *"Health Spheres,"* the United States has a poorer performance record than the other English speaking nations. We are ranked last on most aspects of patient-centered care. It is hard to understand why this is the case since our total spending for medical care is greater than that spent by all of the rest of the world combined. Once again, privatization has not proven itself superior to public institutions.

Interestingly, a recent report indicates the best medical care provided in America is that found in the VA hospitals.

We spend more for health care per person than any other of the developed nations. In 2002, we spent $5,267 per person compared to $2,160 in Britain, $2,817 in Germany and $2,931 in Canada. Our expenditure was 14.6% of our Gross Domestic Product while the United Kingdom spent only 7.7%. For that extra money we get a higher infant mortality rate, higher rates of cancer, diabetes, high blood pressure, heart disease, strokes and lung disease, a lower life expectancy and poorer overall care. The richest country in the world is not the healthiest. The Institute of Medicines estimates there were 18,000 unnecessary deaths due to lack of health insurance in 2004. Well over $120 billion is lost annually in productivity of the uninsured because only 49% of adults receive recommended screening and preventative care.

Right now, our states are having difficulties dealing with the escalating cost of Medicaid and the prospect of the addition of baby boomers is troubling. These costs accounted for about 17% of 2005 state budgets.

The reason for our higher expenditures is obvious. Those other countries provide health benefits to all their citizens while we provide it to those who have insurance or can afford private payment. Ten years ago, Taiwan had a system like ours and abandoned it in favor of the globally more popular government controlled single payer system. This change in their system increased the number of citizens covered from less than 60% in 1995 to over 97% in 2002. According to Health Affairs, this expansion came at virtually no increase in cost other than normal growth that would be expected from income and population growth. Taiwan adopted a system more practical and frugal than ours.

Health care in the United States is a privilege and should be a right. Socialized medicine is anathema to Americans. But, moderates are sensible people and recognize that there are some areas where private enterprise cannot perform like public entities. Why can't they? It is because their motives are in conflict with our objectives – **we have an impractical and adversarial healthcare system.**

The insurance company's motive is to maximize profits and that is best served by fighting to delay or avoid paying medical bills even if they are legitimate. The bureaucracy needed to administer our fragmented system has, by its very nature, higher costs. Most major health insurers spend less than 80% of health insurance revenue providing health care. Medicare spends 98%.

The natural repugnance of socialized medicine has a grip on our cosmetic conservatives – they want to believe against it because it is not *"Laissez-faire."* A single payer system is not socialized medicine, it is communal health insurance. Most Americans acknowledge that Canada and England have far less expensive systems, but they bewail the long waits and lack of certain medical services there. They fail to recognize that the single payer nations provide overall superior medical coverage in spite of the shortcomings. Four of our most conservative values, morality, patriotism, frugality and practicality, demand that we should go to such a plan because it would cover all our citizens and it can be accomplished at little or no increase in cost if Formosa is any indication.

A recent University of California study estimates that the United States could save over $161 billion every year in paperwork alone by adopting a single payer system. **This is a glaring case where realistic conservative values favor a progressive health care program.**

The large numbers of uncovered people, especially the children, are also part of our team; why shouldn't we want to include them in the benefits of being an American? It is the public interest. We are already paying for those uncovered citizens and illegals anyway since they use the free clinics and emergency rooms supported by the public.

Now the drug lobbyists have promoted a federal drug plan that is beyond reason. Our Nonservative leaders ran this bill through Congress in 2003. They claimed it was to provide affordable drugs for seniors, but the apparent real purpose was to pay back the insurance industry, the drug companies and the HMOs for their past election support. The effective date was early 2006 so few looked at it closely. This is the industry charging us a multiple of world prices and some cheating on their taxes – both immoral and unpatriotic.

Outrageously, a provision was included explicitly denying the Medicare officials from negotiating bulk prices from the drug companies. Administration officials claimed that the competitive market place would bring costs down to the lowest possible level. It is not a free market.

Families USA did a study and found that the US Department of Veteran Affairs has negotiated drug prices around 48% below on average the prices for those through the new Medicare drug insurance plan. There are dozens of examples of outrageous price spreads for widely prescribed drugs comparing Plan D with the VA.

A political fabrication is that our Nonservative leaders want a smaller, more efficient government. The facts indicate they really want to use our tax money to reward special interest allies with no regard as to the size of the government's deficit. A party who views government mainly as a vehicle for rewarding special-interest allies rather than serving ordinary citizens, can never be trusted to run government frugally or competently (Lord Acton – *"Every class is unfit to govern."*)

Administration officials decry the *"government price controls"* that negotiated prices would entail. *"We the people"* should decry industry controlled artificial prices a multiple of world prices. Our system is capitalism for the ultimate public good. Where is the public good in this program obviously written to maximize the profits of those corporations who have contributed much to the Nonservative leadership? Negotiated price controls are frugal and practical and are not *"government price controls"* so obnoxious to most people

There must be circumstances where the public's interests come before the profits of price controlling corporations. We abandoned fair business practice laws, but there is nothing fair about offering blatantly lower drug prices in other countries than to Americans. If Congress really had the public interest at heart, this situation could not happen. This is irrefutable proof that our Nonservative leaders are misleading the public as to the masters they serve. To put forth the argument of *"the power of competition"* as justification for significantly higher prices reflects their Machiavellian craving for the enormous campaign donations of the insurance and pharmaceutical industries.

Part "D" has found widespread satisfaction among seniors, but corporate profits for the drug and insurance companies are accelerating and they plan to spend more than $100 million on lobbyists in one year to insure that the plan remains unchanged. **We were told competition would drive prices down, but both drugs and Part D costs to the elderly are increasing.** Who's driving?

A direct government single payer program would be more frugal, practical and efficient as amply demonstrated by the drug programs of other nations. Each of the numerous private insurance plans must carry a profit and the profits are directly dependent on how efficiently the insurance companies impede claims. Who's driving?

The following is a column written by Frank Kaiser for his web site: suddenlysenior.com:

"Shouting from the January 2006 cover of AARP Bulletin is "THE NEW MEDICARE MATH: Cheaper than Canada?"

"Surprise, surprise! It is cheaper, given the distorted numbers AARP picked for its few contrived examples. It is also statistically inept and altogether unrealistic.

"In other words, it lies.

"One example: AARP claims that in New York, a three-month supply of Fosamax (70 mg) costs $413 each under the least expensive Medicare plan, but is $516 from Canada. Check most any Canadian pharmacy site and you'll find that $413 will buy you more than year's worth of that drug.

Who'$ Driving?

"Make no mistake. Seniors don't always get a better deal when buying from our neighbor to the north. In as many as 25 percent of all comparisons between Plan D and Canada, Plan D wins. Especially if your income is less than $1,197/mo. ($1,604 for couples) and you have few assets.

"But why would AARP deliberately deceive us?

"AARP has a nasty habit of loading the dice to favor its position. Back in 2003 it rigged its own poll claiming, "A resounding 75% of AARP members polled in a survey... said that the proposed Medicare (drug) legislation should be passed..." while a USA Today/CNN/Gallup Poll and others showed a large majority of AARP's 37-million members opposed the bill. Over 60,000 members quit in disgust.

"Why lie? Take a look at these numbers, courtesy of Public Citizen.

- "Sixty percent of AARP's revenue comes from selling insurance products and drugs. (Membership dues represent only 29 percent of total revenues.)
- "The largest portion of that comes from the two million AARP members enrolled with UnitedHealth Group.
- "According to a December 21, 2005 press release from UnitedHealth Group, 2005 revenues will be $45-billion while expected 2006 income will increase to $70-billion, a 64 percent increase due, one can assume, to increased revenues from the new Medicare drug plan.
- "Whopping increases in revenue for UnitedHealth Group means the same for AARP.

"Any clearer now?

"We've come to expect Congress and the Administration to lie and pander for the greedy drug and insurance lobbies. That's the Washington culture today. But for an organization that specifically claims as their primary mission "to enhance the quality of life for all as we age," to also bow before the gods of avarice, it is despicable.

"Such blatant corruption is apparently irrelevant to AARP's boss, William Novelli. Founder of Porter-Novelli, a global marketing and public relations firm, the current head of AARP was the author of the pandering and perfidious Harry and Louise commercials that killed "President Clinton's healthcare plan, an initiative that would have avoided today's crisis for seniors as well as our current shame of 47-million uninsured Americans.

114

Who'$ Driving?

"Today's Medicare Reform Bill never should have passed in the first place. No one wanted it except the insurance and drug companies, and their paid toadies in Congress and the White House.

"To get it passed, Congress flimflammed and Medicare lied.

"Not to left out, AARP spent $7-million on TV commercials to convince its 37-million members of the inconvincible: that the Bill was anything but a trillion-dollar giveaway that did little for the average senior, that would cripple our economy, eventually kill Medicare (which AARP, as the American Association of Retired Persons, opposed at its inception), and for which our children and grandchildren would be paying dearly for the rest of their lives.

"At the time, AARP's Novelli tried to reassure members that, although Plan D was far from perfect, there would be plenty of time to repeal its worst aspects and provide a true drug benefit.

"That was two years ago. Has AARP fought in any way for a less expensive, less complicated, and more effective drug bill? You tell me.

"AARP is the second largest membership organization in the US after the Catholic Church. Congress is in awe of this so-called senior advocacy behemoth.

"But instead of fighting for seniors, AARP lies to us, throws us to the HMO wolves, and builds power on our good names. In turn we are rewarded with the occasional hotel discount.

"All of us betrayed, sacrificed in the name of greed."

William McGuire, with more than $1 billion worth of unexercised options, resigned as chairman of UnitedHealth Group (AARP parent) after an outside review of stock-option program concluded backdating was used to maximize profits when exercised. He will receive a $6.4 million lump-sum when he leaves plus an annual pension of $5.09 million. This reward was not because AARP cares about retired people.

Many are finding that they can buy drugs in Canada at great savings over Part D. The CEO of one Canadian pharmacy says demand for Canadian drugs should not drop as long as U.S. prices are about three times the world average price. Unfortunately, the Federal Government has been confiscating drug packages coming from Canada as improperly labeled causing the drugs to not meet FDA standards. The flimsy excuse is that the labeling is improper because it is in both English and French. This is curious since most of these drugs are manufactured in the same facilities as drugs sold in the States. More than likely, the Canadian labels are affixed on the containers there as well.

Who'$ Driving?

Winston Churchill – 1874-1965

"However beautiful the strategy, you should occasionally look at the results." Sir Winston's words deserve our thought. The American medical care is the worst in the western world at greater cost in dollars, lost work and deaths - these results are tragic. In the world of medicine, it may be that *"Laissez-faire"* is beautiful, but America must focus on the results.

The medical field as a whole demonstrates that private industry may well be inferior to a single payer communal system. A report by Consumers Union found that not-for-profit nursing homes generally provide superior care than for-profit nursing homes. They usually have more and better qualified staff so each resident receives almost an hour of additional nursing care every day. Like the VA, this reflects the superiority of communal activity in certain critical areas of human activity. Unfortunately, the not-for-profit facilities account for a small minority of all nursing homes. It is even more unfortunate that virtually all nursing homes do not meet accepted basic care standards.

If the VA and non-profit nursing facilities are providing the best medical care in the nation, it would seem prudent to use these models to provide medical care and drugs to the nation. Medicare is a program widely approved by Americans so we should use Medicare itself as the single payer. It is vastly more efficient than a private insurance plan because Medicare's focus is primarily on patients while private insurance focuses solely on profits.

A recent survey of Canadian residents indicated they are happy with their system run by their government. While elective surgery may be delayed, overall care is superior to ours at significantly lower cost per patient. Why ignore a better system simply because many regard it as socialized medicine? **A single payer system, like Medicare, while not a perfect system, works in the public interest.** Extending that system to cover all Americans would save money, reduce the worry many lower class citizens have over medical costs, and save many lives. This is the apparent choice of the Proservatives.

Who'$ Driving?

If we went to a single payer system, we would add 47 million of our fellow Americans to the coverage. **This includes almost 12 million children – this meets the challenge of our society's morality.**

While you might think that would increase our total medical costs, it would not because most of these people are already receiving medical care at public expense. Coverage would move many treatments from emergency rooms to more effective and cheaper doctor's offices. Also, the doctors themselves would incur great savings dealing with only one payer rather than hundreds of private insurance companies. Based on the experience in other countries, it could actually lower overall costs.

Patriotism, Morality, Frugality, Practicality, and Balance: a single payer system is patriotic including all Americans; it meets the test of American morality by including 12 million children; it is practical and frugal saving billions in administration costs; will help balance the budget; and it alleviates a significant imbalance in our society. **Two of the largest items contributing to our federal deficit are Medicare and Medicaid. By implementing a single payer system, these could be successfully put on a pay-as-you-go basis like Social Security.**

The author admits that this is only one idea for dealing with a complex problem. There may be other and better methods available. It should be apparent, however, that our current system is more than just unsatisfactory. It is not working to the *"General Welfare."*

Sageisms:

"Poverty is the parent of revolution and crime." -Aristotle

"When the doctrine of allegiance to party can utterly up-end a man's moral constitution and make a temporary fool of him besides, what excuse are you going to offer for preaching it, teaching it, extending it, perpetuating it? Shall you say, the best good of the country demands allegiance to party? Shall you also say it demands that a man kick his truth and his conscience into the gutter, and become a mouthing lunatic, besides?" -Mark Twain

"Freedom is a possession of inestimable value." –Cicero

"Government is not reason, it is not eloquence, it is force; like fire, a troublesome servant and a fearful master. Never for a moment should it be left to irresponsible action." -George Washington

Who'$ Driving?

Chapter Twenty-four
Corporate Disasters

Exxon-Mobile earned $39 billion in one year. How is it that the oil industry tripled their profits in just three years? Is it simply because greater demand has coincided with supply not growing quickly enough or is it that we have ignored alternatives?

The answer lies not with oil but with the government which has been silently resisting research into alternate fuels since 1972 - the first oil embargo. They have been resisting, in part, because of the lobbying pressure from the oil industry. Congressional politicians are interested in incumbency and their need for money is provided by big business. They need your votes, but they get those votes through heavy advertising and by misleading the public in areas like this – inalienable political fabrications. There is little real difference in socialist government ownership of the means of production and powerful government avoiding a frugal and practical alternative fuel to protect private interests. *"Exclusive privilege of corporations"* **violates conservative values.**

You will hear a lot of rhetoric about alternate fuels but you will see little meaningful action as long as corporations are allowed to lobby Congress. They lobby to drill more in Alaska and off shore – a stop gap that merely passes the problem down a generation. Why does the oil industry get $4 billion is special indirect tax subsidies every year? Americans need a practical, renewable fuel source as soon as possible.

Brazil embarked on such a plan, 33 years ago, to eliminate their dependence on foreign oil and they are on schedule to accomplish that goal in 2007. Their fuel is now 40% ethanol made from sugar. We could have done that as well. With the technology that has been developed over the last 33 years, mostly by Brazil, we could accomplish the same goal. It probably would not seriously hurt the oil industry, and it would help the sugar and corn farmers, and it just might get them off our Federal subsidy programs as well. Currently there is a 54 cent per gallon tariff on imported ethanol. Who lobbied for that?

The energy required to produce ethanol from sugar is less than one-sixth the energy used to produce ethanol from corn. Also, sugar ethanol reduces greenhouse gases more than corn ethanol. It is the logical choice for both ethanol and for soft drinks. Using sugar without tariffs and import quotas would aid Caribbean and African nations we now subsidize with foreign aid. Ethanol can also be made from switch grass (potentially the best source,) tree limbs, twigs and leaves.

Taxpayers can save four ways – fuel costs, foreign aid, farm subsidies and land fills now used for tailings from the lumber industry. But first, we have to make some basic changes in how the people's business is done in Washington. The CosCons need to recognize that their leadership advocates what is a form of welfare for special interests only. The influence of the oil industry on government is among the worst illustrations of how private interests can work contrary to the *"General Welfare."* Enormous corporate cartels are, by their very nature, potentially disastrous for the consuming public.

Corporate America is never perfect. Examples are Polaroid, United Airlines, Montana Power, Enron, WorldCom and the sugar and corn industries. As indicated before, Americans are second rate as far as the soft drink industry is concerned. Over the long run, the vast majority of corporate business entities ultimately fail. Where is Montgomery Ward?

Polaroid is a recently bankrupted company. Their demise is strictly technology related and may have had little to do with the relative merit of their management. But it is interesting because it displays the disdain our managerial aristocracy and our courts have for others – even long term valuable employees.

The following is an article in The American Reporter:

"COMPANIES REPLACE PENSIONS WITH BROKEN PROMISES AND LIES"
by Randolph T. Holhut, American Reporter Correspondent
Dec. 11, 2005

"DUMMERSTON, Vt.—It wasn't that long ago that the American workplace operated under a simple compact - in exchange for offering your employer 20 or 30 years of your labor, your employer would pay you a living wage and give you a pension when you retired.

"Combined with Social Security and Medicare, this meant that old age was no longer a time to be feared. You could live out your final decades in a certain amount of dignity, knowing that you had enough money to live on and health insurance to cover you when you got sick.

"This system, sadly, doesn't exist anymore for most Americans. The new model of retirement looks a lot like what recently happened at Polaroid."

Unable to adapt to digital imaging and the decline of its instant photography business, Polaroid filed for bankruptcy in 2001. Just before it went bankrupt, the company canceled lifetime health care and insurance benefits for its retirees.

"A group of retirees sued Polaroid to force the company to honor its commitments. They were, for the most part, unsuccessful.

"In April, the remains of Polaroid were sold for $426 million. Polaroid chairman Jacques Nasser (if the name sounds familiar, he was at the helm of Ford during the spate of fatal accidents involving the Explorer SUV in 2000 that ended up costing the carmaker millions in lawsuits and lost sales) will receive $12.8 million for his shares in the company. CEO J. Michael Pocock will get $8.5 million.

"And 6,000 Polaroid retirees will get $47 each.

"That's not a typo. People who worked 20, 30 even 40 years for Polaroid are getting $47 as their "reward" for devoting their lives to a company that kicked them to the curb at the earliest opportunity while handsomely rewarding the people at the top.

"Promises made to workers no longer need to be kept, not if they cut into the fat cats' profits. And the same bankruptcy laws that were recently changed to make it harder for the average person to walk away from debts are allowing corporations to terminate their workers' hard-earned health care and retirement benefits.

"United Airlines is in the process of dumping $5 billion in pension obligations onto the Pension Benefit Guaranty Corp., a federal agency that insures private pensions if companies go bankrupt. Unfortunately, the PBGC faces a deficit of $30 billion and will not be able to handle the flood of companies that will rush to follow United's lead.

"As for United's 120,000 current, former and retired employees, who just saw their pensions disappear, they now apparently have no way to fight this decision. Maybe, if they're lucky, they'll get a $47 check like the Polaroid engineers.

"For all the talk about retirement planning, the reality is that only about half of Americans work for companies offering some sort of retirement plan. Of that number, 80 percent have what's known as defined-contribution plans - the 401(k) system where you are expected to plan and save for your retirement. If you don't earn enough money, or if you get sick or have some other financial crisis in the present that prevents you from saving for the future, that's your problem, not your employer's.

"Only 20 percent of workers who have retirement plans have defined-benefit plans - a pension that the company funds and that promises to pay you a monthly check when you retire. Of those remaining defined-benefit plans, 75 percent of them are under-funded.

"Do the math and you can see what is happening. Fewer people get pensions. Those who now have them stand a good chance of losing them, as companies seek to escape from the promises they once made. Workers are now expected to save for their retirements, but most Americans are in low-wage jobs and are deeply in debt. And the one thing that keeps most retirees from living on Alpo - Social Security - is about to be radically changed so even that guarantee of a stable retirement income can no longer be counted on.

"In other words, the social contract is being rewritten and can be summed up thusly: "You're on your own, pal." If you're among the fortunate few who have money and have invested wisely over the years, you'll be fine." Everyone else is screwed.

"You can't expect to maintain a functioning democracy for long if this is the guiding philosophy. But in the era of President George W. Bush, promises don't have to be kept, commitments can be broken at will and money talks so loudly that it drowns out every other voice of reason and sanity."

Randolph T. Holhut has been a journalist in New England for more than 20 years. He edited "The George Seldes Reader" (Barricade Books).

Two Polaroid's executives get over $21 million for bankrupted shares, regular stockholders get zilch, and 6,000 retirees get a total of about $300,000. Like United Airlines, other huge corporations are dumping their retirement plans on the Pension Benefit Guarantee Corp. – that is *"we the people."* Many others are dropping defined pension plans and reducing medical insurance benefits– for millions of workers.

As United Airlines exits from Chapter 11 Bankruptcy proceedings, the reorganization plan includes an equity incentive program that would award 11% of the new stock issue to 400 of top management and gives $56 million in convertible notes to management employees. It seems the failed management is rewarded with millions while their disappointed stockholders got zero, and their retired employees see benefits reduced.

The Pension Benefit Guarantee Corp. took on $2.9 billion in unmet benefits for 59,000 US Airways employees last year and their exit from bankruptcy was dependent on that. They still have a $5 billion shortfall in their pension fund, yet they can offer $10.2 billion to buy Delta including $5 billion in cash. Management sees nothing wrong with this.

Who'$ Driving?

Montana Power's story is more despicable since technology or other outside sources had nothing to do with its decline. That can be laid solely to their managerial aristocracy. MPC was built as a public utility with legislated guaranteed profits of 13%. It was one of the most stable stocks on the New York Stock Exchange and was valued as a high quality, high yielding conservative stock. Their electric power rates to their customers were among, if not the lowest in the nation.

The beginning of the end started when the legislature passed Senate Bill 390 in 1997, the so-called "Energy Deregulation Bill." It would be interesting to discover who lobbied for this legislation, except it is just too obvious. This blunder was to allow MPC to diversify. Management wanted greener pastures so they could join in the frenzied growth seen in other industries.

Management began to sell off their highly profitable, albeit slow growth assets. Some time prior to these sales Montana Power formed a subsidiary known as Telecommunications Resources Inc. TRI purchased Touch America, allowing expansion into telecommunications and began construction of a fiber-optic network with the intention of going national. Investment banker Goldman, Sachs & Co. of New York was hired to help separate Touch America's telecommunications businesses from Montana Power's energy utilities.

The $2.7 billion from the sale of the utility facilities were spent on installation of 18,000 miles of fiber optic cable in this failed venture called Touch America, which eventually filed for bankruptcy and sold its assets for $43 million to 360 Networks of Vancouver, British Columbia. The sale was handled by Touch America's chief executive officer, Bob Gannon, with the help of New York Wall Street firm Goldman Sachs. The loss was a staggering $2.457 billion. Goldman Sachs was paid $20 million (for their valuable help going broke?) and four executives collected $5.4 million. Then $500,000 additional bonuses were paid to other Touch America managers for a smooth transition into limbo.

That was the end of Montana Power Company. Without any consideration that their stockholder's primary interest was in stability and a very safe generous dividend, management chose to enter into a highly speculative venture. When it didn't work out, management bailed out with a golden parachute and the stockholders got nothing. In addition, residential customers then faced significant rate increases.

That is corporate America at it lowest. Well, almost! Enron, WorldCom and others may hold that distinction. Those stories need not be retold. However, there was legislation passed in reaction to such accounting scandals. The Sarbanes-Oxley accounting law required corporations to make their boards of directors more independent and created new regulations to oversee auditors. The Securities and Exchange Commission also instituted new protections for investors, notably those owning mutual fund stocks.

Our managerial aristocracy is now attacking these new rules as too expensive. One concerns executive stock options being counted as an expense, like other forms of compensation – not counting these increases the bottom line, bonuses and stock options. The SEC has proposed regulations that would allow shareholders to nominate their own candidates for corporate directors. Do we really not have that right? Exactly who's driving these corporations? Is it the stockholders?

All U.S. manufacturing accounts for about 75% of our exports, creates around 15 million jobs, and provides the bulk of research and development. The auto industry accounts for a hefty share of that – more than any other industry. Both GM and Ford recently announced their intention to reduce their work forces by about 25%. Many workers and many more children will suffer.

They, of course, cannot compete because of the labor unions raising their labor costs to a multiple of their foreign competition. However, if the anti-trust laws had been enforced in the 1900s, there might not have been just three, one foreign owned, domestic auto manufacturers. Dealing with multiple manufacturers, the unions might have been less successful and the labor costs might be more competitive. Even post World War II, there were eleven manufacturers. Huge size creates disadvantages for competitors that can be fatal; but can eventually lead to other problems jeopardizing the giants.

A large corporation buying other corporations is a popular, though perhaps misguided, means for growth. Some chief executives focus only on mergers as a means for growth and that virtually guarantees they will have significant failures. Very few such mergers benefit both the buyers and sellers stockholders according to research done by Andrew Campbell and David Sadtler published in *"strategy + business"* issue of 1998.

Their contention is that more corporations can increase stockholder value by breaking up than by mergers. The best example of this is the break-up of AT&T into many parts all of which gained great value. Unfortunately, they are all rejoining. The biggest obstacle is found in management that does not want to reduce their positions of power and potential income. Campbell and Sadtler estimate that $1 trillion of stock value could be gained by broad restructuring into fewer, smaller entities.

Who'$ Driving?

Many very large and successful companies generate large amounts of surplus cash and pay minimal dividends as large stockholders do not want to be penalized by double taxation. The problem of excess cash is solved by purchasing firms in the same or similar business areas. This has the additional appeal of diversifying risk. The problem becomes one of multi-layered management and a loss of focus. In addition, the very top layers, with the greatest expenses, may not have any revenue base.

This can also create large departments with no fiscal restraints. For instance, a computer programming department works only to provide services for the other departments. There is no revenue stream created so the prestige of the department can only be measured in the size of their budget. The manager enhances his position by enlarging his staff while ignoring their efficiency – this actually happened at a major retailer.

Sometimes, those at the top have insufficient knowledge of what is really happening at lower levels. The top levels in any huge corporation have an *"information disadvantage."* Many attempts at bridging these gaps fail. Trying to bridge these gaps can create a deluge of computer information that becomes almost meaningless since the data often is in fields not familiar to top management.

In 1979 Lee Iacocca, who eventually became an icon of American business success, persuaded our government to guarantee over $1 billion in Chrysler debt to help them avoid bankruptcy. There were only five domestic auto manufacturers left (Checker closed in 1982 and American Motors was merged into Chrysler in 1987) and a Chrysler bankruptcy might have devastated their many employees and suppliers. Iacocca did bring the company back, but there was great debate over the success of the loan guarantees.

There is no way to know how different the outcome would have been if Chrysler had simply been allowed to bankrupt; most speculate the difference would have been small. Over 50% of their employees lost their jobs anyway. Mismanagement was the cause of Chrysler's decline into near bankruptcy. Just as Henry Ford's lagging behind in design and engineering dropped him to third largest behind GM and Chrysler in the 1930's, Chrysler's lag post World War II dropped them back to third.

Part of the inducement for the government guarantee was large reductions in Managerial salaries. In 1981, these cuts were restored and about two-thirds of the salary lost was paid retroactively even though Chrysler was still losing money. By 1983, the company returned to profitability and the guaranteed loans were paid relieving the government of potential liability. Part of the profits, however, was the result of wage concessions by the UAW and part was tax loss carry forwards and not actual operating profits so the public did incur a cost.

The business world wants the government to stand aside when they are expanding through merger, but they want government to step in when they are in trouble. This is *"laissez-fair unless we need you."* The business world's side of our two way street must be clear of all obstacles, but they want the right to use our side whenever they want.

If a corporation is highly successful, it gains almost national praise. But success is neither the only nor the best standard. Corporations have responsibility to their customers, their employees, the owners and the public. When a corporation becomes so large that management is insulated from those responsibilities, we witness the special treatment and outlandish remuneration related too often in the press.

In the 1993-1995 periods, stock companies paid their top handful of executives about 5% of profits. By 2000-2002 hoarding increased it to almost 13%. Many of the separation pay packages recently publicized are outrageous. Nardelli leaves with $210 million.

Corporate disasters are a certainty. They will happen because our corporate aristocracies, just like feudal and ancient aristocracies, are just people and people make mistakes. They may be well-intentioned, but that will matter little to the multitude of people hurt. The only way to minimize the damage is to minimize the extent of the disaster by limiting the size of corporations and watching them closely. Certainly capitalism is the best system for most aspect of human activity, but practical observations indicate not for every activity and huge corporations have built-in disadvantages for the lower level employees and the public, in part because huge corporations are not true capitalism. Who's driving?

Sageisms:

"Everyone is always in favour of general economy and particular expenditure." -Anthony Eden

"Power always has to be kept in check; power exercised in secret, especially under the cloak of national security, is doubly dangerous." -William Proxmire

"There is no act of treachery or meanness of which a political party is not capable; for in politics there is no honor." -Benjamin Disraeli

125

Chapter Twenty-five
The RAP Control

The world has seen only a few times when political control was taken from the rich and powerful and handed over to the multitude. Three examples are the Magna Charta, the French Revolution and our own Revolution. In combination, these events led to successful republican forms of government, now referred to as democracies. Other examples were the forced creation of India and Pakistan as democracies, the New Deal, the disintegration of the USSR, the women's rights and black rights movements – among the few examples that were peaceful. Control went into the hands of the many and the results have been spectacular providing the many with a balanced and level playing field.

Mary Wollstonecraft (1759-1797)

Like John Lilburne, Mary is one of the forgotten heroes in the fight for liberty. In 1792, she published *"A Vindication of the Rights of Woman"* which was the first significant treatise in favor of women's liberation. Wollstonecraft preached that intellect will always govern and sought *"to persuade women to endeavour to acquire strength, both of mind and body, and to convince them that the soft phrases, susceptibility of heart, delicacy of sentiment, and refinement of taste, are almost synonimous [sic] with epithets of weakness."*

The corporate aristocracy with the support of the Nonservatives has been chipping away at the political gains we have made. They are supporting changes that hand control back to the rich and powerful. Congress is passing liberal laws designed specifically to benefit and give advantage to certain private sectors. **This enhances the concentration of wealth which also hurts the women's movement because of the** *"glass ceiling."* The shift of income share upwards leaves the women and youth behind. Certainly, the Nonservatives believe that there can be no set of circumstances that would lead us back to little or no freedom. Probably the citizens of Rome felt the same way before Caesar.

Who'$ Driving?

The Administration asks us to support our troops in Iraq and let them fight the War on Terror using tools that infringe on Constitutionally guaranteed human liberties. Those two requests (as concepts) are made up of contradictory or incongruous elements. Are we not fighting that war because of the threat terrorism poses to our liberties? How exactly can we give up our liberties in order to fight for our liberties? Who is wise enough to draw that line? Benjamin Franklin said: *"They that can give up essential liberty to obtain a little temporary safety deserve neither liberty nor safety,"* and Ronald Reagan said: *"There is only an up or down - up to man's age-old dream - the ultimate in individual freedom consistent with law and order - or down to the ant heap of totalitarianism, those who would trade our freedom for security have embarked on this downward course."*

Suspending any one of the Constitutional guarantees built into our system poses a significant threat to the American way. While we must support and respect those on the front line of battle, we must never forget those who were out there in the past. Don't dishonor those who fought and died at Trenton, Yorktown, Gettysburg and across our South, Normandy, Midway, Iwo Jima, the Bulge and myriad of other battles. Abraham Lincoln said at Gettysburg: *"It is for us, the living ... those we here highly resolve that these dead shall not have died in vain."* We should all be alarmed that our Administration has claimed the *"necessity"* to infringe on personal liberty. Many great leaders have warned of this because there is simply no one qualified to draw the line as to what is really *"necessary." "No class is fit to govern."*

Anne-Robert-Jacques Turgot (1727-1781)

Taxes date back to Biblical times and were most burdensome on the common man. Turgot was among the leading economists of 18th Century France and is one of the heroes in the historic fight for liberty. As a chief government administrator in the Limoges region, he found peasants kept only about 20% of their meager harvest – you think your taxes are high! He helped alleviate that situation by cutting taxes and freeing serfs from work obligations to landowners, giving them more liberty. As an inspiration to Adam Smith's free trade and *"Laissez-faire"* economics, some consider him the founder of modern political economics.

Mankind's greatest economic progress parallels that of individual liberty. **Individual liberty parallels the decline in the political control of the rich and powerful.** Once, mankind's riches were measured in land, slaves and serfs all working for the benefit of the upper classes. It was only when the serfs and slaves were freed that enormous progress was possible. Innovation and invention are almost always the brainstorm of the common man.

Many believe that the invention of the steam engine ignited the industrial revolution. This is not so! It was the re-invention of the steam engine in an environment of liberated workers. The first steam engines, more than a thousand years earlier, were only novelties during the Roman Empire because they could not compete with slave labor.

Contributing greatly to this process was the invention of the printing press and movable type. The availability of cheap books hastened the spread of literacy and education of the lower classes. Again, however, it was only possible in an environment of individual liberty. The Chinese had a printing press much earlier, but they have never had liberty.

Some, albeit few, will remember the history of riots and demonstrations by the working class protesting the installation of labor saving devices early on in the industrial revolution. And yet these are the people that benefited most, because it added financial independence to the political freedoms they had already earned. **Ironically, the RAP themselves are now immeasurably more numerous and far better off because of these new liberties and the financial independence of the consuming lower classes.**

History is littered with examples of riots by the neglected lowest class – we have seen it recently in France. Many try to claim that France's recent problem is part of the Moslem terrorist war on the west. More than likely it is a reflection of the disadvantage that those people have in their own society. We saw it here in America when several of our larger cities were torched. The totally obnoxious welfare system was an ill-advised attempt to deal with this problem. The only possible real solution is education and equality of opportunity. We have given them liberty, but we have neglected giving them a chance. They often turn to crime, which reinforces our general disdain and fills our prisons.

The French problem is due in part to the importation of large numbers of Algerians because the RAP needed cheap labor to do the heavy labor the French themselves had outgrown. Does that sound familiar? Early in our history, we imported Africans. Now, we have a large illegal immigrant population greatly troubling our citizens.

Can you realistically believe that we could not stop these immigrants if we wanted? The military has these wondrous night vision and heat sensor devices and could easily close the borders. The RAP reaps enormous rewards from the low cost of employing them. The general public pays a hidden tax providing for their health and education needs. Our government listens almost solely to the demands of the RAP and, so, we have illegal immigrants. What would happen if we shut off and deport illegal immigrants? There are 12 million illegal immigrants in the United States and there are 8.5 million unemployed. Without the illegals, there would be no unemployment. That would put enormous pressure on wages and the rate of inflation.

Every wave of new immigrant minorities is frowned on by the general population. Many believe that families with generations of history here are somehow superior to new arrivals, but that is repeatedly disproved by those with only a few generations of history. The Chinese imported to build our western railroads joined the Irish and Italians as new residents here about 100 years ago and have become thoroughly integrated. The *"Know Nothing"* political party formed in the 1850's primarily to protest the influx of Irish Catholic immigrants. It gained some success and is reminiscent of the anti-Hispanic movement we are witnessing today. This is another prime example of the shortness of man's memories concerning history.

Compare the economics of hiring illegals today with the use of slave labor prior to the Civil War. Illegals are definitely a better deal because of our failed welfare system. With slaves, the owner bore the total responsibility of caring for the slaves. While that care was probably minimal, the owner provided for all their needs. The families of the slaves did not all contribute economically just as the families of our illegals do not all contribute economically.

The employers of illegals have passed the economic cost of the families of the illegals on to the taxpayers. In effect the employers have precise control of their labor costs since there are many illegals available for work at domestically low rates. Their costs are fixed while the taxpayer's costs have no limits.

The children of illegals born in America are U.S. citizens and entitled to all the benefits provided by our laws. The illegals do not have medical insurance coverage so they use the charitable medical facilities available all around our nation. The children are educated by public tax dollars. Admittedly, the owners of the housing occupied by illegals pay school taxes, but most moderates are convinced it is the lowest kind of housing probably yielding less than the cost of the schooling.

The RAP and corporations that employ illegals mostly collect and remit taxes to the government; so many illegals are paying taxes even though they may not file tax returns. It is all the benefits that the American taxpayers carry. The CATO institute argues that they create more wealth than they cost so they are a benefit to the nation. That is probably true, but does not justify the average taxpayer carrying the benefits burden that should be carried by the employers.

However, it is highly likely that the government will continue to drag their heels on this issue because they owe their incumbency to the RAP and corporations. Whether you favor amnesty or tighter controls for the illegals themselves, it is time to recognize who actually is in control of this issue, like most other issues. It is not *"we the people"* and it should be. Where is the balance? Who exactly is driving?

About 5,500 years of history says the rich and powerful gave us little more than wars, turmoil and suffering. Common man gave us progress. We had to have a good deal of freedom before the *"idea of progress"* itself was re-conceived only a few hundred years ago. While some of the ancients wrote of progress (Lucretius and Seneca,) it, like so many other ideas, disappeared with the loss of liberty in the Dark Ages. Humans simply existed and their lot did not improve until the advent of widespread liberty. There is no convincing evidence that human nature has changed or improved so what progress we have experienced must stem from the spread of liberty. **Progress lays, essentially, in the** *"education of the human race"* – St. Augustine

One of the reasons our form of government works so well is found in the checks and balances that limit power. In the past, our huge government has helped power our economy through the redistribution of wealth to the growing middle class. In part, the whole works because the governmental segment is inefficient, and because it limits the control of the rich and powerful.

How do we know that the explosive growth of the middle class and the expansion of governmental power by the masses made the difference? **First, we can see the same process taking place in other nations around the world right now.** That and the internet spreading knowledge around the world should spread liberty, democracy and peace if we can maintain political control here in the hands of the people. Also, we know because it had never happened, on an equivalent scale, before in history. History tends to repeat itself so there is almost never a new paradigm. But, when something really unique happens and it is for the better, conservatism demands that it be maintained.

To be sure, the ancients made great economic and technological strides where some degree of liberty existed. The Greek City States and the Roman Republic are the best examples. However, both had a small middle class and large slave populations. Britain and our Republic were the first and largest with widespread liberty. America also had, more importantly, an ingenious constitution limiting the control of any group of people. Corporations virtually did not exist.

Our governments, on all levels, are really just economic pumps. They collect taxes and pay it all out (and in recent years much more) in their many programs. Sure, there is waste and there is corruption, but all of it flows back into the system. Much of the funds that flow through these pumps go to the middle classes, but an overly disproportionate amount is horded by the rich and powerful. The seemingly wasteful welfare programs are an insignificant part of the total, yet are a major focus of fault finding by the CosCons. Welfare and other entitlement programs may actually establish a cushion under our economy lessening the detrimental effects of recessions.

Thomas Paine said: *"Government, even in its best state, is but a necessary evil; in its worst state, an intolerable one."* Madison's intent in the Constitution was to check the inherent pitfalls found in human nature. Ronald Reagan's conservatism removed the stigma of the pitfalls found in human nature. Individual private enterprise is the basis of capitalism, but it must have an underlying sense of moral values. Does the fact that private enterprise is performing some activity successfully make that activity valuable? **Ronald Reagan made it acceptable for conservatives to approve of the corporate business world living off and growing the government, all the while hating big government.** This distortion of *"Laissez-faire"* allows an *"elastic"* government and is turning control back to the elite. The very rich advocate smaller government publicly, but they don't want to give up the defense budget, the endless pork barrel handouts, and they ignore the deficit.

In Northeast Georgia, the populous is fraught with worry that the government will build a new interstate highway through the beautiful mountains thereby ruining the rural environment. More than likely, Interstate-3 will be built because the RAP will reap enormous rewards from the highway construction contracts. The new transportation bill

Who'$ Driving?

($286 billion) is more than the cost of the entire interstate highway system and these funds will be spent somewhere.

The Federal Budget now is primarily a means to take our tax dollars and pass it out to the special interest groups. Is there a valid measure of their influence? Certainly! Between the years 2000 and 2005, the number of registered lobbyists in Washington has increased from 16,342 to 34,785. These people exist almost exclusively to elicit pork and generate laws providing huge benefits for special interests - proving the RAP do not want balance or a level playing field.

Over that same time frame, the number of *"earmarks,"* increased from 6,073 to 15,877. This is pork barrel funding for *"pet projects."* They are not the "pets' of the congressman, they are the "pets" of their lobbyist's sponsors. **Even Newt Gingrich wrote that politicians now use big government spending to create an insider dominated system in Washington to insure their incumbency and retain control at the expense of good government.**

The Nonservative Congress has authorized enormous amounts of wasteful expenditures. In 2004, Federal subsidies for agriculture increased 40% even though farm income had doubled. About 90% of farm subsidies go to 10% of the farms. CosCons claim they want education left to state and local governments, but a 51% increase in the Education Department's budget just passed. The prescription drug addition to Medicare has a potential liability greater than Social Security itself. The real beneficiary of that plan is the drug and insurance industry – more than likely, their lawyers wrote it. Bush threatened to veto it when there was an attempt to trim its size.

Recent budget cuts hit students hard with a $12.7 billion slash of the loan program combined with higher interest rates and fees; our students were hurt and the banks benefited. Young ambitious students who are incurring debt to gain an education represent the future of our nation. Any program that inhibits this just to benefit the private sector is foolhardy at best. And, in this case, the banker beneficiaries hardly need any help. Our youth needs this help.

The commercial banking industry is a highly profitable industry in America with profits exceeding 18% of revenues. Only Mining, Crude-Oil Production (29.9%) and Internet Services and Retailing (23.8%) were more profitable. Also cut were funds to aid states in collecting delinquent child support and in federal foster care assistance. To hurt our children while helping business is proof the RAP are in control and their actions show little regard for the *"General Welfare."*

Who'$ Driving?

The Deficit Reduction Act of 2005 cut spending on Medicare, Medicaid and education. According to the Congressional Budget Office, 65,000 people, mostly children, will lose health insurance. Leaders say it is necessary to reduce the deficit. What is the public interest? Is this meeting the test of our morality?

These same leaders are trying to repeal the estate tax. This cost will increase the deficit more than four times the savings from the Deficit Reduction Act in just five years even though only one estate in 200 pays any tax now. Lobbying for this repeal has come primarily from 18 powerful business families including the Waltons – inherited wealth – *"wealth without work."* (Gandhi)

The Senate has a rule that any tax bill that would deepen the deficit more than five years hence requires 60 votes for approval. If it will not lead to a deficit, 51 votes are sufficient. The capital gains and dividend tax cuts previously passed under Bush initiative is to expire in 2008 and the extension now proposed would deepen the deficit by about $50 billion over the next ten years. With the 60 vote rule, it will not pass.

Since the RAP will benefit so greatly from this extension, some way must be found to offset the impending deficit addition so it can be passed with 51 votes. They conceived of the new Roth IRA program. Under the current IRA plans, taxpayers deduct contributions in the year made and pay taxes when the savings and earnings on the savings are cashed sometime in the future. The Roth IRA plan turns that around with taxes paid in the year contributed, with no tax due when withdrawn. The benefit is that the Roth IRA will grow tax-free with no tax liability on the earnings in the future.

The net effect is that deposits into the new Roth IRA plans would develop more tax revenue now. This revenue would offset the revenue lost by extension of the dividend and capital gain tax cuts so the combined bill can be passed by 51 votes. The lawmakers chose to ignore the future tax revenue lost on the earnings of the Roth IRA plans. Our Nonservative leaders **deviously circumvented their own rule** so they can extend tax cuts for the RAP amounting to $50 billion over the next ten years by providing another tax benefit for the RAP which could cost billions more in the future. Will this help our kids? **It is not moral!**

An enormous amount of pork was added with no fear the CosCons would react. Tom DeLay even has the nerve to declare that Republicans have cut all unnecessary spending. Can any sensible person believe that? Contractors, performing government tasks in Washington, charge $105 per hour on average – over $200,000 per year per employee.

Who'$ Driving?

The corruption built into this system is again coming to light. Jack Abramoff may be just the tip of the iceberg. It is imperative that the American Proservatives focus on the corrupting influence of the lobbyist system and the immorality that threatens our liberty and system of self-government. **America cannot afford an *"elastic"* government.**

Presidents in the past have vetoed many bills because they contained large amounts of pork. Reagan vetoed 78 bills. The elder Bush, in just four years, vetoed 44. Now, however, the RAP, as the primary beneficiaries, are so confident of their control that our leaders fronting for them no longer even posture an opposition to pork.

George W. Bush has vetoed one bill based solely on his religious beliefs and none on pork. CosCons will argue that he had no need to veto other bills since his party controls Congress. This was also true of Coolidge (50 vetoes) and Hoover (37 vetoes) who presided when the plutocracy created the dangerous conditions leading to the Great Depression. (Eisenhower vetoed 181 bills; Nixon, 43; Ford, 66.)

In our current administration, there seems to be no accountability. The sub-contracting of the war effort in Iraq is symptomatic of this outrage. A similar abuse of power was seen in the clean-up in New Orleans after the hurricane. They can **award huge contracts without bidding,** because the CosCons are fully sold on the big lie. The RAP will make mistakes and *"we the people"* will pay.

Mary Wollstonecraft said: *"An ardent affection for the human race makes enthusiastic characters eager to produce alteration in laws and governments prematurely. To render them useful and permanent, they must be the growth of each particular soil, and the gradual fruit of the ripening understanding of the nation, matured by time, not forced by an unnatural fermentation."*

Arnold Toynbee warned: *"The struggle of men to out vie one another in production is beneficial to the community; their struggle over the division of the joint produce is not. The stronger side will dictate its own terms; and as a matter of fact, in the early days of competition the capitalists used all their power to oppress the labourers, and drove down wages to starvation point."*

This can be seen now in downsizing, outsourcing, exportation of manufacturing, elimination of specific benefit retirement programs, lower support of health insurance programs, the obscene increase in corporate officer compensation levels and corporate profits. These policies are an *"unnatural fermentation"* and simply do not fit into our ideas of what America means. Who's driving?

134

Chapter Twenty-six
Lobotomize Lobbyists

When the RAP get too strong, it endangers the economy. They will make mistake and some will be dishonest – there is no built-in morality in business success or wealth. Bankruptcies of huge corporations reap devastation to retirees, employees and stockholders. The New Deal, anti-trust and fair business practice laws were instituted to limit the control of the rich and powerful, and that still makes sense. These laws need to be aggressively enforced, yet they seem to be hardly enforced any more, and we are continually hearing of giant corporations buying up their competition because, in part, the anti-trust enforcement bureaucracy is heavily lobbied by Corporate America. AT&T is essentially reunited.

Consider the plight of many of our largest corporations right now. There are enormous hidden obligations in under-funded retirement and pension plans. General Motors and Ford are rumored to be on the verge of bankruptcy. The largest airlines are virtually crippled. Where will it end? Social Security, on the other hand is not under-funded or broken. In 2015, Social Security will have a reserve of $5 trillion dollars. Well, it should have except it is being spent and added to our National Debt by our Nonservative leaders (both sides) in Washington – a highly immoral political deception. Will our children have this safety net?

Management's motivation was to take care of themselves and their top employees, but laws were passed, in all fairness, that health care and retirement plans had to include all full time employees' not just management. The generation of the 1930's is now mostly retired in comfort and many in luxury because of these plans. The southern and western states are full of them. Is it possible that the Baby Boomers may miss out on that? The RAP want the Federal Government to take up the slack and assume the retirement obligations of the failing corporations.

But that is typical. Greg Palast said: *"In the deregulated market, profits are privatized and losses are socialized."* **In any situation, when governments use contractors, there will invariably be corruption. Also, it is highly doubtful if they can do it significantly cheaper because of the necessity of making a profit.**

Corporations are *"persons?"* Lincoln said: *"government of the people, by the people, for the people, shall not perish from the earth."* We all agree that is what America is about. Realistically, it now reads: *government of the people, by the corporate persons, for the corporate persons."* Senator Henry Fountain Ashurst said: *"When I have to choose*

Who'$ Driving?

between voting for the people or the special interests, I always stick with the special interests. They remember. The people forget."
 Our democratic system of *"Separation of Powers"* can perish because people forget. The concentration of wealth accelerates because people forget. Remember what Reagan said: *"We the people" tell the government what to do, it doesn't tell us. "We the people" are the driver, the government is the car. And we decide where it should go, and by what route, and how fast."* We must not allow the corporate lobbyists and their campaign contributions to run our government. Again, the difference between run and ruin is the smallest of letters. It is not just: *"Who's driving,"* it is *"Who the hell is driving?"*

Sageisms:

"People never lie so much as after a hunt, during a war or before an election." -Otto von Bismarck

"The basis of a democratic state is liberty." -Aristotle

"Controversial proposals, once accepted, soon become hallowed."
-Dean Acheson

"Important principles may and must be flexible." -Abraham Lincoln

"Politics have no relation to morals." -Niccolo Machiavelli

"Millions of innocent men, women and children, since the introduction of Christianity have been burnt, tortured, fined, imprisoned; yet we have not advanced one inch towards uniformity. What is the effect of coercion? - to make half the world fools and the other half hypocrites."
- Thomas Jefferson

"A tyrant must put on the appearance of uncommon devotion to religion. Subjects are less apprehensive of illegal treatment from a ruler whom they consider god-fearing and pious. On the other hand, they do less easily move against him, believing that he has the gods on his side."
-Aristotle

"Politics and the pulpit are terms that have little agreement."
-Edmund Burke

Who'$ Driving?

Chapter Twenty-seven
Terrorism

**Alexis de Tocqueville
(1805-1859)**

Alexis de Tocqueville's admiration for our system inspired his treatise *"Democracy in America"* in 1835. De Tocqueville compares America to Europe by comparing the merchant seamen of both. The European is consumed by fear, returning to port when the unexpected occurs; while the American is fearless in the face of any danger. Americans have a consuming need to accomplish their goals.

While we have lost many of the qualities that de Tocqueville so admired, we still have the boldness that was birthed by liberty. We will take risks and we accomplish more than most if not all. We lead the world. We are the biggest and the best by far. So, why then, do so many around the world frown on us; and why do so many others even hate us?

Maybe it is because, as the biggest and the best, we always believe that we are right. We have an unyielding sense of perfection; we won't drink French wine because they dared to disagree with us (forgetting that we might have lost our Revolution without France.) How dare anyone criticize us? After all, aren't we the most generous, giving people that have ever lived? Haven't we always, in times of world crisis, gone to the aid of others, laid down our lives, sacrificed fortunes, and maintained their liberties? Maybe, it is because we have an inborn need to act quickly and decisively, perhaps before we have fully considered the complete situation and evaluated the potential consequences.

Proservatives believe they are entitled to open and truthful information from political leaders. Local government independence and fiscal responsibility are among their highest values. Social and economic justice is also highly valued as are peace and civil liberties. All citizens have the right to be heard with respect for their opinions. Can anyone question that most administrations in the past respected these values? When private phones are tapped and internet communications monitored, such actions violate our basic values. The claim of *"necessity"* is not sufficient justification because there can never be sufficient justification.

137

Who'$ Driving?

What we are witnessing now is not the real America and this is not a war on terror. Wars are openly fought. Nor can there be a war on terror since terror is no more than a word describing a heightened fear. The expression *"war on terror"* is a slogan, a political device meant to keep the populace in an excited fear. **We are morally obligated to protect the liberties of our children.**

Adolph Hitler used such slogans effectively: *"you must harp on these slogans until the last member of the public understands what you want him to understand by your slogan."* Now our Nonservative administration uses the slogan *"war on terror"* to maintain their control. Past administrations have used *"war on poverty," "war on drugs"* and *"war on crime"* in the same way.

Terror as an extreme political tool is pervasive in history. The First World War was precipitated when Gavrilo Princip assassinated Archduke Franz Ferdinand. About 30 years ago, the Baader-Meinhof Gang in Germany and the Red Brigades of Italy terrorized those nations. We had our Oklahoma City bombing, the Olympics bombings in Atlanta and the clinic bombing in Birmingham. There is no known effective way to combat terrorists other than the way the Italians and Germans dealt with their terrorists - hunt them down and bring them to justice.

The IRA terrorists eventually disintegrated because their victims choose to ignore them, and their fellow Catholics finally expressed general disapproval. In the end, terrorism is a futile tool for the terrorist, but a useful tool for the political leaders of those terrorized.

Hitler used an act of terrorism to justify suspension of civil liberties and fomented a hysterical hatred of Jews and communists. His rhetoric was not aimed at Germany's enemies. It was aimed at his own people to solidify his political position. The leaders of some Islamic nations and Muslim terrorist leaders use similar slogans to foment political unrest and hatred against Israel and *"imperialist"* America. Unfortunately, we have reinforced that unrest and hatred with our continuing actions in both Afghanistan and Iraq where many innocent bystanders are being killed. **Terrorism will last as long as there is prejudiced knowledge and significant inequities in the world.** If you would fight a war on terror, these must be your targets and your weapons must be education and opportunity. **Any traditions, religions, institutions and social classes that impede education and opportunity jeopardize the *"Separation of Powers"* and individual liberty.**

Many must have a troubled feeling that we acted too quickly in Iraq based on incomplete and misleading information – the threat of

Who'$ Driving?

"Weapons of Mass Destruction" and ties to Bin Laden. Both proved to be questionable, so the rationale of invasion became the effort to rid the world of a tyrant and bring democracy to the Middle East. Saddam is gone and they have had their elections. **Why are Americas finest still there fighting and dying in their civil war?** The election of 2006 expressed widespread voter's disapproval.

Many have a further feeling that if we had expended all the resources and manpower to successfully chase down Bin Laden and his gang, we would have not sacrificed our prominence in the eyes of the world. Saddam would have continued his brutal ways, but the Iraqis probably would have incurred far fewer casualties, the area would not be so unstable, and we would not have lost so many of our own youth.

Diverting our attention to Iraq from hunting down and punishing Bin Laden and the Taliban who protected him was a serious error. We had widespread World support, and we could have rebuilt Afghanistan into a **model democracy inspiring the rest of the Moslem world.**

Isn't that really what we needed to accomplish? Isn't that the real America? We can counter the external threat to liberty by making sure the world knows that, as a matter of national policy, we will not tolerate terrorism and will go to any lengths to punish the terrorists. We will lunch our fastest fleet, brave any storm and hunt them down. They will know there is no safe haven and they will think more than twice about attacking us. John F. Kennedy said: **"Let every nation know, whether it wishes us well or ill, that we shall pay any price, bear any burden, meet any hardship, support any friend, oppose any foe to assure the success and survival of freedom."** That is the only realistic way to fulfill our moral obligation to protect our children from terrorism.

Sageisms:

"In order to become the master, the politician poses as the servant."
-Charles de Gaulle

"Perhaps it is a universal truth that the loss of liberty at home is to be charged to provisions against danger, real or pretended, from abroad."
-James Madison

"In a country well governed, poverty is something to be ashamed of. In a country badly governed, wealth is something to be ashamed of."
-Confucius

Chapter Twenty-eight
The Public Interest

Not so many years ago, the citizens served by the Detroit Edison Company happily paid what amounted to the highest electric power rates in the nation. They did that because Detroit Edison operated in the public interest. Consider that when your electric stove malfunctioned, a Detroit Edison repairman would come to your home and fix it. The charge for labor and parts was zero. That's right – no charge! If your electric dryer broke, they fixed it. Any major electric appliance was repaired in your home at no charge. If a small appliance ceases to work, you would take it to the local Detroit Edison office and then pick it up a few days later good as new – no charge. It gets even better – just save up your burned out light bulbs, take them to Detroit Edison and get new ones free. That is the public interest.

Of course, Detroit Edison is a public utility company and had legislative authorization to earn a reasonable profit on their activities so they were amply compensated for this terrific service in the higher electric bills. Everybody was happy. That is the public interest. Then the U.S. Supreme Court heard CANTOR vs. DETROIT EDISON CO., 428 U.S. 579 (1976) - No. 75-122 - argued January 14, 1976 - decided July 6, 1976. A local druggist doing business as Selden Drugs Company stocked light bulbs but sold few, so he took Detroit Edison to court for restraint of trade under Federal anti-trust laws.

The end result was that Detroit Edison Company customers no longer received free light bulbs and appliance repairs at no charge. The lawyers got very rich (triple damages) and hearsay is the druggist went broke. He got his wish to sell light bulbs, but his customers disappeared in their justified anger. Sometimes, it would seem reasonable that the public interest should be taken into account. There is no question that the druggist should have the right to sell light bulbs. On the other hand, there is no question that a public utility company is there to serve the public interest as prescribed by law. *"However beautiful the strategy, you should occasionally look at the results"* - Sir Winston Churchill.

There are industries whose basic businesses are so closely intertwined with the public interest that suitable controls by the public are demanded. The justification for this can be found in our basic beliefs and the Declaration of Independence: *"We hold these truths to be self-evident, that all men are created equal, that they are endowed by their Creator with certain unalienable Rights, that among these are Life,*

Who'$ Driving?

Liberty and the pursuit of Happiness. — That to secure these rights, Governments are instituted among Men, deriving their just powers from the consent of the governed, — That whenever any Form of Government becomes destructive of these ends, it is the Right of the People to alter or to abolish it, and to institute new Government, laying its foundation on such principles and organizing its powers in such form, as to them shall seem most likely to effect their Safety and Happiness."

In our modern society, the public utilities and the insurance, power, medical and drug industries can and do directly affect our right to life and our pursuit of happiness. When a focused pursuit of profits has a detrimental effect on the public interest, we have the right and the duty to institute controls because of our moral obligation to our children. We are seeing the hardship foisted on many by excessively high fuel and heating costs, and on some by excessively high drug and medical costs.

We are seeing the drug and insurance industries using their political clout to foist an excessively burdensome health care system on the American public. Other countries have proved their national health care systems not only have better results than ours, they cost considerably less. Our system of *"Separation of Powers"* is breaking down because the RAP and religious right, with the extensive system of lobbyists, may be dominating all three branches in addition to our state governments.

This is not advocating public ownership; it is advocating the need of closer public control for moral, practical and frugal reasons. It is not a blanket condemnation of certain segments of our capitalist system; it is advocating the supremacy of the public interest in all aspects of our American system. Corporations and huge family fortunes may last for centuries, but the public interest will last as long as liberty lasts. **In all of history, whenever private interests reigned supreme, that could be maintained only through feudal power suppressing personal liberty.**

Sageisms:

"I have no fear that the result of our experiment will be that men may be trusted to govern themselves without a master."
-Thomas Jefferson

"Republics end through luxury; monarchies through poverty."
-Montesquieu

"It is dangerous to be right when the government is wrong." –Voltaire

Who'$ Driving?

Chapter Twenty-nine
Thoughts

In dealing with the three fears of our founding fathers, the only way we can limit the power of the government is to put it back in the hands of the people. We must heed Eisenhower's warning: *"In the councils of government, we must guard against the acquisition of unwarranted influence, whether sought or unsought..."* The following are steps that all American Proservatives should demand in the interest of maintaining liberty, the *"Separation of Powers"* and capitalism.

We must return to a strict interpretation of the *"General Welfare"* clause. Line item veto and an Amendment barring deficits are necessary. Gerrymandering must be curtailed – it benefits only political parties.

We must ensure that no person, real or artificial, can seduce candidates with large campaign contributions. All contributions could be made directly to the candidates election fund itself through a public agency and should be limited in size by contributor. There should be no discretionary party funds obligating candidates to party leaders.

The only way we can deal with the threat of a united Christianity is to educate our populace in the dangers of theocracy. We can easily see the evidence of other nations that are dominated by one religion. While religious domination probably will not happen here, some powerful people want it to happen and are working toward that end.

An important step in the restoration of the *"Separation of Powers"* must be the Amendment to our Constitution so badly wanted by Jefferson and Madison. Corporations must be denied the natural rights of citizens – they are not *"persons."* They should not be allowed to own stock in other corporations and there should be no interlocking directorships. They must be held to the higher standard of service to the public good, and all should be treated as if they were public utilities. Charters should be issued only in rare cases where a proprietorship of a partnership will not suffice. We need to restore balance.

Interstate and international corporations doing business in America must be closely supervised by the Federal Government. If your business is here, charter here. Any attempt by a corporation, its officers, directors or major stockholders to influence elections, elected or appointed officials should cause the corporate charter to be revoked and the assets liquidated. Corporate avoidance of taxes should be a criminal offence.

There should be no limited liability of the corporation, its officers, directors, outside paid accounting firms and large shareholders. If a corporation should be in the effective control of one person, that person should be individually liable for the debts of the corporation and criminally liable for any such acts. We should make an effort to reduce the size of corporations by breaking them into geographic and industrial pieces. This can be accomplished easily by a highly graduated tax system. They want the law to treat them as people; tax them as people. They will disintegrate in their rush to save taxes.

There is no evil in corporate size alone. Some achieved dominance simply by being better. Examples are Ford, Alcoa and Microsoft. It is when competition is simply bought out or forced out through unfair pricing practices that the public interest may not be best served. Certainly, when corporations use their financial muscle to influence law enforcement and politicians, the public interest is compromised.

As far as agricultural subsidies and tariffs are concerned, we only need to end them. It could be done in slow stages to minimize the harm to the producers; and it should be done from the top subsidy recipients down. It could quickly and easily be accomplished by converting our power sources from oil to ethanol.

The medical industry may not be a problem in and of itself. It is the insurance companies serving as middle men. There is an easy solution here because many other nations have better medical service evaluations with significantly less cost. Our representatives should investigate those and adopt the best to our system. Why should Americans accept second class medical care and pay more than everyone else? What does frugality and practicality have to say about this? Where is the balance?

Of the four depressions experienced in our Nation's history, three were the direct result of bank failures. The fourth, and worst, was exacerbated by New York bankers controlling the Federal Reserve. **There is something inherently dangerous in great size for banks.** The problem lies in the potential for failure. It may seem difficult to contemplate, but breaking up these enormous corporations should be considered. A return to the geographic limitations of the past should probably limit the potential damage. If a major bank fails, the public will end up with the bill just as we did with the Savings and Loan disaster in the 1980s. We must keep in mind not only our own history of bank failures but those in Japan. The second largest economy in the world was seriously debilitated by those near failures.

Many powerful nations have lost wars to insurgent gorillas. Britain lost the Boar War, Russia in Afghanistan and we lost in Viet Nam. There are many today that feel we may be losing in both Afghanistan and

Iraq. Unfortunately, those in political control rarely, if ever, are willing to admit an error. There can be no question that they will make mistakes, but it may be political suicide to admit it openly. We may now be sacrificing our children's bodies and lives for what history may well view as ill-advised at best.

Teddy Roosevelt said *"We should speak softly and carry a big stick."* It must surly be beyond our capabilities to fight small gorilla wars around the world. Even the strong are vulnerable to invisible foes. We have the armaments but not the incentive to risk massive personnel. What we should do is let the world know of our big stick and that we will not tolerate war or terrorism. If you mess with us, or if you aid and protect someone who messes with us, we will come to you and remove the violating leadership; and then we will promptly leave you alone.

Social Security is not broken ($1.7 trillion of our National Debt is the Social Security Trust Fund) but retirement plans in general need revision. Changing to stock market based savings is simply too dangerous for the average man. Look how poorly the company sponsored stock retirement plans of Enron and other giant companies worked out. Look how huge corporations are wiping out their retirement plan obligations in bankruptcy court.

That program can be improved by reinstating the universal draft. Every able bodied citizen could be required to serve for a specific period of time and retirement benefits will be dependent on that service. The difference between this book's plan and the universal draft of the past lies in when the citizen serves. There will be a choice to serve for a few years early or as a career in the military, police, etc., or late in the civil service for a few years. Placement can be determined by a civil service board using personal choice, education and achievement levels as standards. As most professional civil servants and contractors are phased out, we will incur enormous windfall budget savings and certainly reduce corruption – this duty to participate (like the Athenians) by all citizens in the government should also help alleviate the epidemic public political apathy. According to the Heritage Foundation, 80% of federal revenues are used to administer its own programs. We can reduce that hugely.

Perhaps the most important step in the restoration of our *"Separation of Powers"* must come in our tax system. If Will and Ariel Durant are correct, and concentration of wealth amounts to the *"natural"* result of *"democracy"* and *"liberty,"* then there is only one proved way to avoid that concentration - reviving highly graduated *"equality of sacrifice"* income and estate taxes to achieve balance.

Who'$ Driving?

Alan Greenspan, chairman of the Federal Reserve Bank, said: *"Ultimately, we are interested in the question of relative standards of living and economic well-being. We need to examine trends in the distribution of wealth, which, more fundamentally than earnings or income, represents a measure of the ability of households to consume."* Balance not only insures the integrity of our system, it creates greater and more consistent potential for prosperity.

Henry Ford doubled his worker's pay and everyone benefited. The New Deal spread the wealth and everyone benefited. The greatest progress in history was made under a steeply graduated income tax. Based on the theory of *"equality of sacrifice,"* it is the most fair. What more could one ask of a system of taxation? Take the burden off the high spending middle class and the economy prospers. If a steeply graduated tax, heavy taxation on corporations, excess profits tax, and heavy inheritance taxes will curtail the concentration of wealth, then we need them simply because: *"Every class is unfit to govern ... "*

There may be no clear or present danger, but history says there is always danger. Liberty and progress result from the spread of education and ideas. The least we can do for future generations is to ensure they will have a *"rule by the many, who are neither wealthy nor poor, in the interests of the whole community."* These ideas are truly conservative and realistically progressive insuring liberty for our children. *"We the people"* must drive because *"The test of the morality of a society is what it does for its children."*

Pure

You are as one with the world
as from the womb you uncurled
Same with all that swim, run or fly
Fidelity in all that you try
In all you taste, new surprise
Drinking fully with open eyes
Touching and reaching to feel
Consuming as mysteries unreel
Alive with a need to explore
Abound with a heed to adore
Blessed saint, open and free
As every other child, pure poetry

Chapter Thirty
Conclusion: *"No Left Turns"*

Many will doubt there is any real threat to liberty because it is so basic to our national mindset; but there is no practical way of predicting what the future will bring. It my not be your liberty at risk; it is the liberty of your grandchildren or theirs or theirs. Many, very smart people (names highlighted below) have warned of potential dangers; and their astute observations are in our memories because they earned our respect and their place in history. Our Conservative Standards are their legacy.

Aristotle said: *"The basis of a democratic state is liberty."* **Cicero** said: *"The welfare of the people is the ultimate law."* Special interests, by definition, conflict with the public interest since *"no class is fit to govern."* – **Lord Acton**. Children, the aged and the infirm are not special interests; they fit strictly into the *"General Welfare."*

A government that prostitutes itself to bankers by cutting budgets supporting student loans, and denies graduates from refinancing student loans a second time or from bankrupting such loans, reduces aid to agencies collecting delinquent child support, allows 12 million children to be without health insurance, and runs enormous deficits is an immoral, Nonservative government that does not understand that America is about the children. The morality of our government has been buried under an avalanche of lobbyist funding required by aspiring and incumbent politicians. This transitory influence is not in the *"general welfare."*

Programs enhancing education and health benefit all. **Dietrich Bonhoeffer** said: *"The test of the morality of a society is what it does for its children."* We must meet the measure of our morality as a nation. The public interest must come before any special interests. **Thomas Jefferson** said: *"Educate and inform the whole mass of the people.... They are the only sure reliance for the preservation of our liberty."* The welfare of America starts with and is for the children. **John Ruskin** said: *"The first duty of government is to see that people have food, fuel, and clothes. The second, that they have means of moral and intellectual education."* We need to return to basics with a heavy emphasis on *"consumer-side"* economics, education and opportunity.

History has demonstrated that certain objectives can only be reached communally. CosCons decry communal activities as socialism or, at least, too liberal. That position would have made them Loyalists during our Revolution since revolution is a basic communal activity, as is law and order, charity and even patriotism. Communal activity does not

146

conflict with *"Laissez-faire"* – it is an entirely different realm *"for the people."* *"Laissez-faire"* is only a basic tenant of our capitalist system and it must be subservient to our six basic conservative values.

"The budget should be balanced, the treasury refilled, public debt reduced, the arrogance of officialdom tempered and controlled, and the assistance to foreign lands curtailed, lest Rome become bankrupt." Over two thousand years ago, **Cicero** spoke words that Regan could have said twenty yeas ago. We need politicians to step forward now, not just to say these words, but to implement the *"General Welfare."*

Politically, we have become confused because of the rhetoric of our major parties. The Republicans have laid a claim on conservatism that is patently untrue and has become inalienable. The reckless spending and foreign policies of our Nonservative leaders belie their claims. They are neither frugal nor practical; thus, the Republican Party is liberal and cannot, in any way, be regarded as conservative.

Corporations are judged solely on a standard of success – which also happens to be the basis of Machiavellian politics – ethics and morals can be set aside to achieve success. All corporations are creations of man – they do not have divinely given inalienable rights. They should be held to a higher standard than success – **Adam Smith** said that standard should be *"the public interest."* Supporting Corporate America, based on a standard of success only, does not make sense even if you disregard history, and such support, in light of our conservative values, is *"liberal"* since it is *"not narrow in bounds, opinion and judgment."*

The Republican Party represents those segments of our nation that have historically proved to be unfit to rule – the religious traditionalists and the rich aristocracy whose transitory motivations of self-interest conflict with the public interest. Being pro-active Corporate America, there is a distinct possibility that Republicans are now too closely tied to the rich and powerful, the corporate aristocracy and the lobbyists to realistically defend the liberties of our children through our Conservative Standards. They represent a dangerous imbalance.

The Democrats, on the other hand, continue to spout the same tired rhetoric of their *"liberal"* agenda, such as minimum wage, jobs, the poor and disadvantaged, environmental problems and inequities. They base strategy on issues, like the environment, using unconvincing arguments. They appeal to a standard of *"fairness,"* when there can be no such standard. A strictly interpreted *"General Welfare"* standard alone has validity. To be sure, the above issues are important, but the rhetoric is old and the solutions continue to be elusive.

Who'$ Driving?

Most of these issues can be addressed through steeply graduated income and estate taxes because the *"equality of sacrifice"* system of taxation is a great and impersonal leveler, expanding the consuming middle class. **Aristotle** said: *"The most perfect political community is one in which the middle class is in control, and outnumbers both of the other classes."* Based on America's own historical experience, there is social and political balance only in unbalanced taxation.

As a practical matter, there are only two effective political parties in America. For certain, there are many single purpose parties like the Greens and Libertarians. There is little prospect that any will gain national dominance. This leaves our moderates with a problem. The *"conservative"* label of the Republican Party is very appealing, but a political fabrication. The *"liberal"* label of the Democratic Party is distasteful because of corrupted interpretations of *"General Welfare."* Proservatives seem to choose a party essentially based on opposition to the other party, and they waver back and forth between the two.

CosCon Republicans and LamLib Democrats must examine their positions, challenge their leadership as too corrupt (*"arrogance of officialdom"*- **Cicero**) and liberal, and must rededicate themselves to the true conservative standards of this nation. Most CosCons and LamLibs are really Proservatives loyal to one party or the other because they want to believe the slogans spewing from corrupt political leaders and they blame the other side for our nation's problems.

Ronald Reagan said: *"... we have to choose between a left or right, but I would like to suggest that there is no such thing as a left or right. There is only an up or down ..."* Well, there is a left and a right, but the way is muddied and the pavement has deep and dangerous potholes caused by corrupt and inalienable political fabrications. We have embarked on a downward course because we have forgotten history and are neglecting our Conservative Standards and Values.

Those claiming to be on the *"right"* lie; they make left turn after left turn while their depth perception has worsened and traffic is fast and furious. They are removing or ignoring many of our own proven traffic controls, like anti-trust laws, and it is even more dangerous to make left turns. We need to get off the road and consult our map, we need to remember history, who we are, what we are doing, how we got here and where are we going; and we need to make sure that *"We the People"* are driving watchfully so the children will be safe.

America must return liberty to the top of the list of conservative standards. The struggle to maintain liberty is no more than combat to limit the power of those that govern. The struggle to limit the power of those that govern is no more than combat to limit the concentration of wealth in few hands. The struggle to limit the concentration of wealth in few hands may be no more than combat to maintain a proved tax system insuring balance and a level playing field.

Still, our way has to be a two-way street created morally, practically and frugally. The most practical choice for Proservatives now is to return to the Party that gave us the definition of conservative in the first place. But only if that Party itself vows a renewed commitment to our highest standards. We must rein in corporate power, we must solve our broken medical system, and we must return to a highly graduated income and death taxes for the sake of balance and the *"General Welfare."*

We must show the world our American commitment to peace, civil liberties, social and economic justice, the environment, morality and human rights. We must bring to mind the forlorn little girl with a Star of David sewn on her dress and demand that the world end war and curtail the massive production of munitions. We must set the example because we are America and we love all children.

Lord Acton told us: *"Every class is unfit to govern."* No matter the special qualification of any class, they will be unable to subjugate their private interests to that of the people. **John Adams** said: *"Power always thinks it has a great soul and vast views beyond the comprehension of the weak."* **Arnold Toynbee** said: *"The stronger side will dictate its own terms; and as a matter of fact, in the early days of competition the capitalists used all their power to oppress the labourers, and drove down wages to starvation point."* **Andrew Jackson** said: *"It is to be regretted that the rich and powerful too often bend the acts of government to their own selfish purposes."* That is why our Founding Fathers protected us with the *"Separation of Powers."*

Every historic democracy came to an end. **Plutarch** said: *"An imbalance between rich and poor is the oldest and most fatal ailment of all republics."* **John Adams** said: *"Remember, democracy never lasts long. It soon wastes, exhausts, and murders itself. There never was a democracy yet that did not commit suicide."* **Montesquieu** wrote: *"Republics end through luxury; monarchies through poverty."* In his farewell speech, **Dwight Eisenhower** said: *"In the councils of government, we must guard against the acquisition of unwarranted influence, whether sought or unsought, by the military industrial complex."* **Ronald Reagan** said: *"Freedom is special and rare. It's fragile; it needs protection."* America must be ever vigilant: *"that this*

Who'$ Driving?

nation, under God, shall have a new birth of freedom - and that government of the people, by the people, for the people, shall not perish from the earth." – **Abraham Lincoln.**

Thomas Paine said: *"He who would make his own liberty secure must guard even his enemy from oppression; for if he violates this duty he establishes a precedent that will reach to himself."* That is why real American people were given the *"Bill of Rights."*

Ronald Reagan said: *"Ours was the first revolution in the history of mankind that truly reversed the course of government, and with three little words: "We the people." "We the people" tell the government what to do, it doesn't tell us. "We the people" are the driver, the government is the car. And we decide where it should go, and by what route, and how fast. Almost all the world's constitutions are documents in which governments tell the people what their privileges are. Our Constitution is a document in which "We the people" tell the government what it is allowed to do "We the people" are free."* Who the hell is driving?

America is a widely diverse community dependent on liberty, democracy and capitalism to achieve the greatest *"General Welfare."* The world is slowly joining us in these highest values. Whether you use a car or a horse as a metaphor, man's mode of transportation through time is society. Without liberty, the car will not hum and the horse will not sing.

Man, in slavery and servitude, has spent over 5,000 years teaching our horse to sing. Make very sure that the children will always be able to sing the lyrics, which vary from country to country around the world, but carry the same vital message: *"Let freedom ring."*

America

My Country, 'tis of thee,
Sweet land of liberty,
Of thee I sing.
Land where my fathers died,
Land of the pilgrim's pride,
From every mountainside
Let freedom ring.

Rev. Samuel Francis Smith

Epilog

Echoes Most Dear

Starts with one thought: *"I think, therefore I am"*
What is it about? Life cannot be but a sham
Once we all hunted, then we began to farm
Grow, invent create, defend ourselves from harm
Industry, technology and physiology came to know
A clue there, we can't know why, our job is just to grow
We hear and read stories of this god and that
Who's way is better, man's past one long spat
Herded in space and in categories as well
We earned a chance when we learned how to spell
Listen, talk, learn our world, speak and hear
Flag of peace not furled, discard now our spear
Knowledge compounding, so very complex
The knowledge of man, a fast growing text
Divisions abound in all our complexity
In guideposts of life, we need just simplicity
Knowledge, communication making our world small
We need understanding, tolerance for and by all
On the stair of evolution, we are more than a pawn
Look to our great teachers, where have they gone?
They went up in smoke on the wind and in ground
Little left, maybe some old bones somewhere around.
Left echoes over the ages, echoes we need hear
Pillowed on the long reach of time, echoes most dear

God bless America.

Who'$ Driving?

From **Nursery Rhymes for Old Farts**
Art by Mary Harlan

Sideways:
Life should not be a journey
To the grave on a hospital gurney
With the intent to arrive well preserved
And all of your potentials conserved
Rather slide in sideways with a smile
As with everything, do it in style
Beer or Champagne in your hand
Singing along with your favorite band
Thoroughly used up and worn out
Go out with a loud joyous shout
Begin and end with a nursery rhyme
And make sure to have a super good time

Crackerjack
I find the more I give
Of unconditional love to friends
The more I have to give
And the serenity that love lends
Each time I give some away
That much more surely comes back
No limit on hugs every day,
Each hug a sweet crackerjack.
No bottom to that box
Taste all I can and still have more
In love's joyous paradox
Peanuts and prizes galore

Peace
It is very easy to keep our marriage conflict free
Though under my breath I may tell her to go fly a kite
I never fail to let my old bag correct me
Especially when there is no doubt I am right

Peanut Butter
Late in life, sex is like Skippy
Still it's better than when it was Jiffy

Lost in Thought
Quick as a wink
I stopped to think

Who'$ Driving?

Campbell Allen Harlan, Jr. has lived in most parts of our country at one time or another form his birthplace in Detroit, to Madison, Wisconsin in the Midwest, to Ithaca and New York City in the northeast, to Bremerton and Silverdale in the northwest; from Florida and Atlanta in the southeast to Phoenix in the southwest and New Orleans in the deep south. His father's roots were in Tennessee and his mother's in Michigan and Ontario, Canada.

Just like his father, Cam fathered five sons and each of his sons has two sisters. Both lost a third infant daughter. History repeats!

Cam's life in the work world ran the gamut from truck driver to entrepreneur. He has left his mark on mankind by introducing the first hand puppet golf head covers to the golf industry. While he credits their invention to Karen Craven (known to some as Madonna's high school cheerleading coach) with an assist from Barry Breman (known to some as the Great Sports Imposter) Cam's "Little Bits Company" was the first manufacturer, marketing under the brand name "Club Lovers," and the logo inspired his wife Mary's art work in this book. You cannot go onto a golf course today without seeing some hand puppet golf head covers.

Cam is a concerned citizen and not a professional writer. He apologizes for the repetitions and many errors (such as the lack of footnotes and references) that may infringe on normal professional standards.

Fin   Quick as a blink,
I stopped to think
of our world on the brink
this time, with no wink.

153

Printed in the United States
74134LV00002B/1-99